How Not to Read the Bible

An Authentic Catholic Approach to Scripture for Today

Scott Lewis, SJ

NOVALIS

PAULIST PRESS
New York / Mahwah, NJ

© 2019 Novalis Publishing Inc.

Cover design and layout: Audrey Wells
Cover image: iStock

Published in Canada by Novalis

Publishing Office
1 Eglinton Avenue East, Suite 800
Toronto, Ontario, Canada
M4P 3A1

Head Office
4475 Frontenac Street
Montréal, Québec, Canada
H2H 2S2

www.novalis.ca

Library and Archives Canada Cataloguing in Publication

Title: How not to read the Bible : an authentic Catholic approach to scripture for today /
Scott Lewis.
Names: Lewis, Scott M., 1948- author.
Identifiers: Canadiana 20190119314 | ISBN 9782896886296 (softcover)
Subjects: LCSH: Bible—Study and teaching. | LCSH: Bible—Reading.
Classification: LCC BS587 .L49 2019 | DDC 220.07—dc23

Published in the United States by
Paulist Press
997 Macarthur Boulevard
Mahwah, NJ 07430
www.paulistpress.com

ISBN 978-0-8091-5503-3 (paperback)

Library of Congress Cataloguing-in-Publication Data available on request.

Printed in Canada.

We acknowledge the support of the Government of Canada.

5   4   3   2   1   23   22   21   20   19

Contents

*To the memory of my parents,
Ray and Kay Lewis*

Introduction

A World without the Bible

Imagine a world in which there was no Bible. I visited such a place over 25 years ago. The country was Albania, shortly after the fall of the Stalinist regime. Albania had been an officially and militantly atheistic state. Churches, Scriptures, and any form of worship were forbidden. Simply possessing a bible could earn a person a ticket to a brutal labour camp or even a firing squad.

As I spoke to groups of young people, they started to ask questions. Bibles had begun to flood the country, and although the youth were confused, they were excited and thrilled to be able to pray and ask religious questions. They asked about God, Jesus, sin, salvation, ethics – all starting from a clean slate. They asked in anxious voices about "the sin against the Holy Spirit, for which there was no forgiveness." They were worried that perhaps they had already missed the boat. Not to worry, I assured them: whatever that sin might have been, they were not responsible, since they had not known about it.

I returned to Albania several times over the years, and the situation was different each time. It was a difficult transition for the people – there were no real structures, institutions, or leaders. Western consumerism had arrived with a vengeance.

Everything was for sale for the right price. But most distressing was that the arrival of bibles and representatives of various churches brought some division and theological friction as ideologies competed in that tiny country. Catholics, Evangelicals, Jehovah's Witnesses, and other groups vied with Greek Orthodox and Muslims. Walls between groups grew. Religion began to assume its familiar role as the source of group or tribal identity, and as so often happens, various interpretations of the Bible were pressed into service. There were plenty of bibles to read and individuals ready with interpretations, but not all of them were helpful.

That defines our problem: merely reading the Bible without the proper disposition and guidance can be less than helpful and, in some cases, even destructive. The real problem isn't the Bible, but our misguided interpretations. Far too often, the Bible becomes a weapon in our hands that we use to beat others over the head – mostly those who disagree with us or are different in some way. It is important for us to read, interpret, and apply the Bible in a way that is enlightening, liberating, and positive in every sense. Only then can its illuminating and transforming power be released to do its work. The Bible is a beautiful and holy book when it is treated with intelligence and respect, and that includes the willingness to question and struggle with it.

> The real problem isn't the Bible but our misguided interpretations.

The Bible is probably the most influential book ever written. Today, many homes have a bible, even if it is never read. For centuries, monks copied the entire Bible by hand, hunched over small writing desks without proper lighting, heat, or creature comforts. From time to time, they wrote complaints in the margins of their manuscripts that survive to this day, describing aching backs, numb hands, and failing eyesight. But they believed their discomfort was worth it. They were doing something for God and humankind by proclaiming God's word in written form. The pages were often adorned with beautiful illuminations (coloured designs and illustrations); some of the finest examples are the Book of Kells (in Ireland) and the Lindisfarne Gospels (in Scotland). Some Bibles were bound in covers of silver with inlaid precious stones. The Bible was an object of devotion, but also the source of all wisdom and life guidance. It has sustained countless people in their darkest and most painful hours.

> The Bible, which was written in Hebrew, Aramaic, and Greek, has been translated into over 600 languages. The New Testament has been translated into more than 1,500 languages. The Bible is the top-selling book every year.

The Bible was a key element in the creation of Western culture. It has inspired great works of art – paintings, sculpture, stained glass, and more – most of which are still with us. We can call to mind Michelangelo's *Pietà*, as well as the story of the creation, fall, and redemption depicted on the ceiling and walls of the Sistine Chapel at the Vatican. So much of our classical musical, poetry, and literary tradition was inspired by biblical themes, such as the psalms, the laments, and the passion of Christ. The King James translation, from the early 17th century, has transformed many aspects of our culture.[1]

The King James translation of the Bible did much to form our language. Its evocative language and graceful cadences have found their way into our literature and even our everyday speech. This translation has given us Milton's *Paradise Lost*, John Bunyan's *The Pilgrim's Progress*, Handel's *Messiah*, and "The Gettysburg Address." Many people today use biblical expressions and themes, often without knowing their origin. The first few verses of Genesis were read by the *Apollo 8* astronauts as they orbited the moon on December 24, 1968. It would be very difficult to imagine what our history and culture would be like if the Bible had never existed.

But there is a dark side to the biblical tradition. Along with the many blessings it has brought, the Bible has incited fear, intolerance, bigotry, pain, and bloodshed. The Bible – or at least people's misunderstanding and misuse of it – has been one of the factors leading to wars, persecutions, pogroms, crusades, and the demise of Indigenous peoples and cultures. It has also generated much fear and shame, ironically driving people away from God rather than into a deeper relationship with God. Questionable interpretations of Scripture have saddled people with practices and regulations that are a burden. Differing interpretations of biblical passages have created division and fuelled wars of religion. Those on the wrong end of a biblical interpretation often found themselves in the hands of the Inquisition, which sometimes resulted in imprisonment or death. William Tyndale was burned at the stake in the 16th century for the unspeakable crime of translating the Scriptures into English.

Interpreting the Bible as science has played a large role in rupturing – perhaps beyond repair – the relationship between believers and the scientific community. The story of Galileo (1564–1642), an astronomer and physicist, is a devastating example. He challenged the ancient model of the universe that placed the earth at the centre, with the sun and planets orbiting it. Rather, he stated, the earth orbits the sun! At his trial, Galileo was accused of teaching a cosmology that deviated from the revealed truth of Scripture. He was forced to recant his views and spent the rest of his life under house arrest. Galileo was exonerated only during the pontificate of Pope John Paul II – 300 years later! In 1925, a teacher was put on trial and convicted in Tennessee for teaching evolution. This was the infamous Scopes "Monkey Trial," in which two great lawyers, Clarence Darrow and William Jennings Bryant, were locked in rhetorical combat. The trial was a cultural and religious battle between modern science and traditional ways of interpreting the Bible. It was also instrumental in the rise of the fundamentalist movement in the United States.

Quoting the Bible out of Context: A Double-Edged Sword

The violence, bigotry, intolerance, and hatred of the last few decades, much of it fuelled by religious zeal, drive home a warning for our time. It is said that the Bible kills and gives life; wounds and heals; builds up and destroys. This all depends on who is doing the reading, the personal and collective baggage they bring to the text, and what they think they are reading. We can no longer afford the dubious luxury of reading our Scriptures in a way that is uncritical, uninformed, and unreflective. The peace and survival of our societies and the world just might depend on it.

> It is said that the Bible kills and gives life; wounds and heals; builds up and destroys. This all depends on who is doing the reading, the personal and collective baggage they bring to the text, and what they think they are reading.

This point was well illustrated in a recent controversy. In June 2018, U.S. Attorney General Jeff Sessions created quite a storm by quoting from the New Testament. He was speaking to a mixed group of law enforcement officers about the government's immigration policy: in particular, the separation of children from parents when families tried to enter the United States illegally. In defending government policy, he referred to an infamous biblical passage: "Illegal entry into the United States is a crime – as it should be," he said. "Persons who violate the law of our nation are subject to prosecution. I would cite you to the apostle Paul and his clear and wise command in Romans 13 to obey the laws of the government because God has ordained them for the purpose of order." (The passage in question, Romans 13:1, reads: "Let every person be subject to the governing authorities; for there is no authority except from God.")

The response was swift and for the most part negative – even from many conservative Christians. Many pointed out that in the very same chapter, Paul insists that "Love does no wrong to a neighbour; therefore, love is the fulfilling of the law" (Romans 13:9-10). This same principle is reflected in the Great Commandment given by Jesus (Mark 12:28-34; Matthew 22:34-40; Luke 10:25-28):

"Hear, O Israel: the Lord our God, the Lord is one; you shall love the Lord your God with all your heart, and with all your soul, and with all your mind, and with all your strength. The second is this, 'You shall love your neighbour as yourself.'"

This is merely a repetition and reaffirmation of Deuteronomy 6 – the core of Israel's covenantal theology – and Leviticus 18. In fact, there is a consistent tradition in Scripture of protecting and caring for immigrants and foreigners:

"When an alien resides with you in your land, you shall not oppress the alien. The alien who resides with you shall be to you as the citizen among you; you shall love the alien as yourself, for you were aliens in the land of Egypt: I am the LORD your God." (Leviticus 19:33-34)[2]

Romans 13 has a long and sad history; having Jeff Sessions cite it was in keeping with this dark tradition. In 1850, the *Fugitive Slave Act*, with the support of Romans 13, bound citizens to return runaway slaves to their owners. As recently as the 1980s, the arguments of some Reformed Christians in favour of apartheid in South Africa were based on the Romans 13 principle. Finally, inspired by Romans 13, many churches in Nazi Germany threw their support behind the regime.[3]

Quoting passages from Scripture out of context for one's own purposes is a long way from making a careful, informed application of biblical principles. Unfortunately, the first approach is far more common, from both conservatives and liberals.

Slaves, [Do Not] Obey Your Masters

When Africans were first brought against their will to North America, slave owners were comforted by scriptural assurances that good slaves obeyed their masters. Slaves were present in the Old Testament – Hagar the mother of Ishmael was a slave, for example. Paul advised those who were slaves at the time of their calling to remain so, and his letters to the Colossians and the Ephesians told slaves to obey their earthly masters. Interestingly, Paul states in several letters that in Christ, there is no slave or free person, Jew or Gentile, male or female. But slaves in the southern United States, reading the same Bible, were enthralled by the God of Israel. After all, it was this God who freed the Hebrew slaves. The liberating God of Exodus became a vital part of the African American spiritual tradition.

How can there be such inconsistency and ambiguity in what we call the word of God? Much depends on the one doing the reading. Our reading of Scripture is coloured by our social class, gender, geographical location, and how privileged our lives have been. A white educated European or North American male might understand Scripture differently from people who have been colonized or women who have been dominated. A person living in poverty will read the passages in which Jesus shows mercy to the poor in a different way from a CEO earning an ample salary and huge bonuses. No one approaches the Bible innocent of biases, prejudices, or presuppositions, so it is both helpful and liberating to become aware of our own baggage.

The Bible is an ambiguous book, especially if we read it on a superficial level and without an adequate understanding of the text. This very same Bible has been used to support slavery and abolish it; support war and promote pacifism; oppress women and the poor and liberate them.

The Bible is much more than a checklist of rules, commands, and forbidden deeds. It must be, even though it contains many of those things. A.J. Jacobs, a quirky American writer, decided to live as literally as possible according to the Bible for one year. With gentle, respectful humour, he shows in his 2007 book *The Year of Living Biblically* that this is impossible. Even the most conservative reader makes compromises and adaptations. We do not stone our neighbours to death for blaspheming, nor do we require those with bodily discharges to undergo rites of purification or ring a bell. We do not (or should not) regard people as unclean and untouchable just because of the group they belong to.

What we do find in both testaments is a vast storehouse of collective human wisdom, together with what has been revealed through God's messengers. The result is a kind of instruction manual for humanity. When we immerse ourselves in this wisdom, we have the recipe for a fruitful and happy life.

In the pages that follow, we will examine some of the pitfalls of biblical interpretation. Chapter 2 will begin by tracing the history of the Church's relationship with the Bible, and then explore some key concepts and the nuances of the term "word of God." We will then apply these concepts to the Old Testament (in chapter 2) and the New Testament (in chapter 3). The conclusion will offer a way for us to read the Bible and incorporate it into our spiritual life to promote an encounter with Jesus, the Word of God.

1

The Bible Through History: The Evolution and Development of Biblical Scholarship

A word is not a crystal,
transparent and unchanged;
It is the skin of a living thought,
and may vary greatly in colour and content
according to the circumstances
and the time in which it is used.

—Oliver Wendell Holmes[1]

O ver the centuries, the Roman Catholic Church has enjoyed a rather ambiguous relationship with the Scriptures – what we call the Bible. It is one of the books most often purchased, both for Catholic and non-Catholic households, but possibly the least read and least understood. Often, when it is read, it is done in a superficial or uninformed way. But in either a direct or indirect way, it colours our religious consciousness for good or ill. The roots of the Church, like those of a tree, have drawn sustenance from the Scriptures for its liturgy, spirituality, and religious consciousness for almost 2,000 years. Its easy availability to all, however, is a relatively recent event. In the Middle Ages, books were rare, very expensive, and in most cases, read only by monks, nuns, and priests. Mystery plays, stained glass windows, and popular devotions taught people what they knew of the Bible stories, but with a large dose of fantasy and legend.

The printing press and the Reformation of the 16th century caused an explosion of the publishing of bibles throughout the Catholic world. Up until then, bibles had been painstakingly copied by hand, with each copy taking a year or so to make. Only the ecclesiastical elite and the clergy had access to most of them. Now, bibles were affordable and plentiful, and translations began to appear in the language of the people. Religious tracts supporting one position (and undermining others) were printed and distributed by the thousands. The creation of the internet in our own day can help us comprehend the world-changing nature of the arrival of printing to spread information. The two warring sides in the Reformation debate appealed to the Scriptures. Protestants used them to show how the Catholic Church had corrupted the original message of Christianity. Catholics used it to justify the religious structures and practices of the day, to prove that things had been this way from the beginning. Of course, as is usually the case, neither side was entirely wrong – or entirely correct.

Over the next 300 years, millions of bibles were printed. For many families, it was the only book they owned. This is the stage of biblical interpretation that we call 'pre-critical.' The Bible was read literally: people thought it explained almost everything about the origin of the world and humanity, and the doctrines and practices of the Church.

The Text: Much More than Meets the Eye

In the 19th century, new forms of analysis or criticism developed in universities and soon began to be used widely. Criticism is not meant in a negative sense – it means a particular approach to the text or a reading strategy: for example, historical studies of the Bible, the study of various traditions, archaeology, culture and anthropology, and the study of literary forms. (We can use more than one of these at the same time.) Each approach tells us more about the people who wrote it and their times.

Catholic Bible scholars embraced these new tools. It looked as if we would enter the 20th century equipped to keep up with new developments in the biblical field. But this was not to be. The new approaches undermined some of the long-standing ideas that people felt sure of, such as who the authors of the biblical books were and when they were written. In a fearful defensiveness in the face of modernity at the turn of the century, many theologians and Bible scholars were silenced. In the ensuing Modernist crisis, the great Dominican biblical scholar Père Marie-Joseph Lagrange of the École biblique et archéologique française de Jérusalem was one of the first targets. Others followed; as late as the early 1960s, two professors at the Pontifical Biblical Institute in Rome were silenced for claiming, among other things, that the Book of Isaiah was written by three different authors over a span of 200 years. (Nearly all scholars today agree with them.) The higher forms of criticism were severely limited; some were even banned. This situation lasted almost 50 years.[2]

Pope Pius XII set Catholic biblical scholarship on the road to freedom in 1943 with his encyclical *Divino Afflante Spiritu*.

In it, he encouraged the use of linguistic, cultural, and historical approaches to Scripture, as well as fresh translations from the original languages to replace the very tired and, in many cases, inaccurate Latin Vulgate translation.

> The Vulgate Bible was translated, mostly by St. Jerome, a biblical scholar, from the original languages into Latin in the fourth century. ("Vulgate" means "common version".)

The Second Vatican Council (1962–1965) repeated much of the traditional view that the Bible was inspired and without error. But the Council added an important point: to understand the original message, readers had to understand the literary forms used and the authors' mentality and worldview. Catholic Bible scholars quickly became leaders in this research and were highly respected in their field. The Pontifical Biblical Commission published useful guidelines for studying Scripture. Many Catholics began to study the Bible formally, as well as in workshops or in their parishes. A real interest in the Bible was kindled among Catholics, but this interest has cooled recently. Some people think that analyzing the Scriptures is good for taking things apart and explaining, but does not nourish our spirituality and give life to the Church.

The latest in biblical scholarship has been taught in seminaries and theology schools for the last 50 years, and yet very little of this information has reached the people in the pews. Some express shock and dismay when they hear critical views of the Bible for the first time. They ask, "Why haven't we heard this before?" or say, "This isn't Catholic!" Who is to blame for this state of affairs? Often, clergy resist new ideas or don't take the time to make sound biblical theology available to parishioners. Sometimes the people in the pews resist these ideas because they threaten a person's lifelong understanding, shaking their faith foundations. The readings may not be broken open for the people of God in homilies in a way that gives them life and hope. Preaching can focus on a few hot-button issues, such as abortion or same-sex marriage, no matter what the readings for the day are. When people don't learn about developments in our understanding of the Bible, everyone suffers. The life of the Church is made poorer, and the roots of the tree begin to wither. Our faith has nothing to fear from the truth: we do not need to flee from honest questioning and research.

> The latest in biblical scholarship has been taught in seminaries and theology schools for the last 50 years, and yet very little of this information has reached the people in the pews.

Far too many Catholics know next to nothing of Scripture other than what they hear at Mass. Some other traditions have done a better job of helping the faithful to explore the Bible and use it as a guide for growing in their moral and spiritual life.

Over the years, I have heard many older Catholics say that when they were younger, they were forbidden to read the Bible. Although that was not actually the case, Bible reading was not encouraged. Church leaders feared that individual interpretations might turn into heresy. Even when reading the Bible was "allowed," people understood that the Church – usually "Father" – would tell them what it meant.

Inspiration, Inerrancy, and the Word of God

A bumper sticker I see from time to time reads, "God wrote it; I believe it; that settles it!" In this worldview, the Bible is the inspired and infallible word of God. It means what it says: our role is to read and obey. That doesn't leave much room for discussion! This attitude plays into the hands of those who would like nothing better than to portray the Bible as a relic of the past and religion as an ignorant and dangerous way of life. But the Bible is more complicated – and interesting – than such a superficial and uninformed approach suggests.

If you have ever been puzzled by contradictions in the Scriptures (there are many), or the problems that arise from a literal reading of the Bible, then come with me as we explore the many aspects of inspiration, inerrancy (lack of errors), the word of God, and what the Bible is and is not. Here are a few points we'll look at:

> ➤ How should we study Scripture?
> ➤ What do we need to know before we open the book?
> ➤ And isn't the Bible the inspired word of God? Why do we need any interpretive tools?[3]

Is the Bible Inspired?

Yes, the Bible is inspired, but what does that mean? The view of inspiration that lasted from the early Church until the modern era was that the evangelist or writer was taken over by the Holy Spirit and took dictation from God, word for word. He (and as far as we know it was always a he) was little more than God's secretary. One of the results of this understanding is inerrancy – the idea that Scripture cannot contain any errors, even in the details. Every word is dictated by God, is literally true, and has equal weight. An extreme form of inerrancy is at the heart of biblical fundamentalism.

The Spirit of God definitely blows through the pages of the Bible, but inspiration is always mediated by human consciousness, culture, worldview, historical events, and, unfortunately, the darker corners of the human mind and heart. The Bible is a mix of the divine and the all too human. Passages that are uplifting and sublime may be nestled within passages that speak of murder and mayhem. At times, human emotions, hatreds, fears, and limitations cloud the brilliance of the revelation.

Over the centuries, the traditions that make up the Bible have passed through countless hands. Many have left their handprints in the form of their fears, power struggles, and concerns. There are historical and scientific errors – a demonstrated fact.

> The Church still teaches that the Bible is inspired and contains no errors, and rightly so. But today we would add that the inspiration or inerrancy of a text does not mean that the Bible contains no errors in its scientific or historical details. Instead, what is spiritually necessary for humane living and for salvation contains no errors.

The Bible will not lead us down the wrong path. It will light the way to God if we approach it in a spiritual, intelligent, and informed manner.

We often want to cut and paste passages from the Bible into our own time when it suits us. People have been cherry-picking passages to prove doctrines or theological arguments for generations. But we are usually not aware of the vast distance of time, culture, and worldview that separates us from the world of the first-century Mediterranean, in which the New Testament was written, or the millennia before Christ that generated what we call the Old Testament. What are we to make of Saint Paul's passage commanding women to keep their heads covered while prophesying, because of the angels? Do we worry every evening that it might be the world's last night and that Christ will return tomorrow? Do we believe (hopefully not) that those who do not share our faith are bound for hellfire and damnation? Do we own slaves or look upon slavery as something normal? We must recognize what is transcendent and perennial and what is rooted in and conditioned by a particular time, place, and culture.

Seeing how the principles found in the text play out in the 21st century is challenging. We need imagination, patience, and humility. We cannot simply cut and paste the first-century situation into our own time, but neither can we just shrug and turn away.

How Can the Bible Help Us in This Quest?

There are no quick and easy answers, but we can keep some basic principles in mind before we open the cover and begin to read.

When we call the Bible "the word of God," this does not mean the words on the page.

At Mass, at the end of the first or second reading, the lector says, "The word of the Lord." At times, the priest will use incense on the lectionary (the book of readings used in the Mass). We could get the impression that the word of God is the book and the words on the page. A recent Vatican document, *Verbum Domini* (which means "word of God"), noted that "word" means "communication" or "message," and can take many different forms.

"Word" is a metaphor for the creative and dynamic will of God. The beginning of John's Gospel reminds us, "In the beginning was the Word, and the Word was with God, and the Word was God." Jesus is the Word made flesh. Creation, the events of salvation history, the lives of holy men and women and prophets, the Scriptures, music, art, literature, and poetry – all these qualify as vehicles for God's word. When people stand in the Sistine Chapel and gaze up in awe at Michelangelo's story of the creation, fall, and redemption, they are moved and inspired. God's word has been communicated to them. The Word is the message that God embeds in the medium, rather than the medium itself. In the Eastern Orthodox tradition, artists do not *paint* an icon, they *write* an icon. The medium is a visual depiction of a holy personage, but it also contains a theological message – the word of God. In the same way, the Bible is the catalyst – the receiving of God's Word – and is not directly linked to the exact words on the page.[4]

The purpose of Scripture is not to lay out Church doctrines or structures. Scripture is not a theology textbook or toolkit. It is a record of a people's encounter with God over centuries, with all its light and darkness (the story of the Jewish people in the Old Testament), and describes the experiences of a group of people who journeyed with the most extraordinary person who ever lived (the story of Jesus and his followers).

The Bible should come with a warning label on the cover. *Warning: Misreading this text can cause confusion, intolerance, ignorance, and even violence.* To avoid this danger, let's look at a few ways we should *not* read the Bible.

The Bible Is Not a Scientific Book, and We Should Not Read It That Way

We do not go to a math or physics book for poetry, entertainment, or spiritual inspiration. Likewise, we should not turn to Genesis or any other book to look for a scientific description of the creation of the world and the origins of the human species. Genesis was never intended to be a scientific treatise on the origins of the world. We know from scientists that the earth is billions of years old, not thousands, and that evolution is more than a theory – it is a fact. We need to adjust our understanding of the form and process of God's creative energy in creation, as many theologians have done.[5] Creation must be explained in the language of the 21st century, not that of the ancient Near East in the second or third millennium BCE.

These facts do not stop fundamentalists from insisting that the text is literally accurate. The Creation Museum in Kentucky states that it "shows why God's infallible Word, rather than man's faulty assumptions, is the place to begin if we want to make sense of our world." The museum offers a stunning and technologically sophisticated presentation of one key principle: that the Bible text, especially the Book of Genesis, is literal, scientific fact. This museum says the earth was created in six days, and is only a few thousand years old; evolution is false. An exhibit shows humans and dinosaurs co-existing on an incredibly young planet earth. (In fact, dinosaurs became extinct 65 million years ago, while humans are a very recent addition.)

Does that mean Genesis isn't true? The answer is that Genesis teaches theological truth rather than scientific truth. The theological truth is that God was the original spark of energy that set the universe in motion, creation is good, and we are to care for it. Evil was not God's design, but results from humans turning away from God and pursuing their own ways. Genesis isn't a geology, biology, or anthropology text: there was no Garden of Eden, and no people named Adam and Eve. We are not being punished because someone ate an apple 8,000 years ago. Our theologies cannot be based on a literal reading of Genesis, because it is far too narrow to help us encounter God.

> Genesis teaches theological truth rather than scientific truth. The theological truth is that God was the original spark of energy that set the universe in motion, creation is good, and we are to care for it.

St. Augustine of Hippo, writing in the fourth century, had some wonderful advice: don't say stupid things about Scripture, especially on scientific matters.

> Usually, even a non-Christian knows something about the earth, the heavens, and the other elements of this world, about the motion and orbit of the stars and even their size and relative positions, about the predictable eclipses of the sun and moon, the cycles of the years and the seasons, about the kinds of animals, shrubs, stones, and so forth, and this knowledge he holds to as being certain from reason and experience. Now, it is a disgraceful and dangerous thing for an unbeliever to hear a Christian, presumably giving the meaning of Holy Scripture, talking nonsense on these topics; and we should take all means to prevent such an

embarrassing situation, in which people show up vast ignorance in a Christian and laugh it to scorn. The shame is not so much that an ignorant individual is derided, but that people outside the household of the faith think our sacred writers held such opinions, and, to the great loss of those for whose salvation we toil, the writers of our Scripture are criticized and rejected as unlearned men.[6]

What do we mean by "truth"? Karen Armstrong, an author and religious thinker, speaks of two distinct but complementary ways of arriving at the truth: *mythos* and *logos*. Both are essential, but each has its distinct competence.

The primary way of searching for truth is the mythic (*mythos*). Its realm is that of meaning and dealing with what is timeless and constant. It deals with questions that people have asked for thousands of years: about the origins and meaning of life, the foundations of societies and cultures, pain and suffering, and death. *Mythos* is rooted in the unconscious, the deeper levels of the mind, so this type of truth cannot be rationally proven. "Myth" is not a bad word. In popular culture, it means something that is not true or doesn't exist, but in the world of biblical studies, it means a metaphorical and symbolic way of expressing profound truths.

Logos is rational, scientific, pragmatic. It is concerned with facts, the external ("real") world, innovation, and the future. But it cannot answer ultimate existential questions or soothe pain and sorrow.

When the roles of *mythos* and *logos* become blurred or they are applied incorrectly, serious problems arise. It is not possible to answer existential questions adequately using science or reason. When we try to do this, the result is often clashes and negative reactions. In the same way, we cannot answer scientific questions or make policy decisions using a mythic approach. If we do, we end up with educated people seeing all religion as backward and dangerous, and people who are fundamentalists seeking to turn back the clock and silence all disagreement.[7]

This is good advice for approaching the cultural wars we are engaged in, as well as for dealing with the challenge of evolutionary and materialist views of the universe. The world's best scholars have shown that when it is properly understood, the Bible and modern science can co-exist.

The Bible Is Not Historical in the Modern Sense

The Bible does contain history, but history means something very different in our time than it did in the ancient world. The ancients were not obsessed with facts, as we are. They certainly believed in truth, but truth was not always found in a collection of factual details. For instance, modern scholars agree that the worldwide census that Caesar Augustus ordered in Luke 3 could not have taken place when Quirinius was governor. The only recorded census took place in 6 CE, so the birth of Jesus could not have happened then. Also, Matthew's version of the birth of Jesus placed his birth during the reign of Herod the Great, who died in 4 BCE. Both accounts cannot be literally, historically true. Modern people can find these inconsistencies troubling, but an ancient author would have shrugged his shoulders. Both Luke and Matthew had theological and literary reasons for placing the birth of Jesus at those times. They were not concerned about what information would have been on Jesus' birth certificate, if he had one.

History in the ancient world was written for moral instruction and teaching. Histories highlighted the virtues, accomplishments, and courage of generals, statesmen, and philosophers, and the message was always clear: this is someone to admire and emulate. "Bad" individuals were often mirror images of the heroes. People were urged to reject these examples. Histories were often written by new regimes to justify their rule and authority; we find this in 1 and 2 Samuel. In other instances, previous kings were presented in the worst possible light. We see this in some of the Old Testament historical books, such as 1 and 2 Chronicles, which condemn the reigns of many of Israel's kings.

An obsession with proving the factual or historical nature of Scripture, and the insistence on reading it only in a literal way, is fairly recent. This approach came out of 19th-century historicism and obsession with objective facts. The Church Fathers, although they began by reading literally, saw this as only an outer shell. They insisted that Scripture was a bottomless well that could be continually plumbed for moral and spiritual insights. The presence of something ridiculous or unworthy of God or one of God's messengers was seen as a red flag, telling the reader that the true meaning must be found below the upper layers.

The Church Fathers based their interpretation of Scripture on the elasticity and the boundless depths of the text. For instance, most readers would find Numbers 33:1-49 rather boring – it lists the different places where the Israelites camped on their journey out of Egypt to the Promised Land. But a Church Father named Origen (185–254) built a rich spiritual and theological treatise on these passages. He teased out the root meanings of the Hebrew names of the stages of the journey. It became a description of the spiritual life and journey of the soul. The Church Fathers were comfortable using symbols in the Old Testament that foreshadowed Christ and the Church. In 1 Corinthians 10, Paul speaks of the journey of the Israelites through the sea as a type of baptism, and the rock that followed them through the desert to provide them with water as the presence of Christ. Most important, the Church Fathers were not afraid to use the imagination to create a spiritual consciousness. Chapter 3 will explore how to use your imagination in reading and meditating on biblical passages.

For Further Reflection

1. What is your understanding of how the Scriptures are inspired? How does this influence your reading of the Bible?

2. "It is important for us to read, interpret, and apply the Bible in a way that is enlightening, liberating, and positive in every sense." Why is that so important? How do we do this?

3. Think of a time when you had a conversation with someone who had a very definite interpretation of a scripture passage and would not listen to any alternative understanding of that passage. How did you respond to this way of thinking?

4. Do you ever find yourself responding to Scripture in a dogmatic or narrow-minded way? Has this chapter given you a broader point of view?

2

The Old Testament: A Rich and Diverse Library

The Old Testament plays a key role in our ongoing culture wars. One major issue is the collision between the biblical account of creation and the findings of modern science. Add to that questions of sexuality, gender relations, marriage, capital punishment, abortion, and war, and the Old Testament can become a battleground.

Even in translation, the writing is at times incomprehensible. The worldview of the writers is far removed from our own, and the things that the characters in the stories take for granted are sometimes shocking and disturbing to us. We do not practice slavery or polygamy (at least legally), and sacrifice – animal or human – is not part of our religious practice. We would not consider one hundred foreskins a suitable gift from a man to his prospective father-in-law to seal a marriage proposal (1 Samuel 18:20-30). We would not think that the fact that a ruler had called for a census of the people made him worthy of divine punishment in the form of a plague (2 Samuel 24:1-25). We are not familiar with talking serpents (Genesis 3:1-5) or donkeys (Numbers 22:27-30), or staffs that turn into serpents (Exodus 4:1-5). Many people turn away from the book, often with a negative opinion of the Old Testament, and sometimes its God and people. Others insist on its literal truth, painting themselves into an intellectual and religious corner that helps no one.

But we do need to understand what the Old Testament is – and what it is not. It is a collection – a library – of many religious writings from various historical periods. This library includes laws, creation myths, poetry, prophecy, history, legends, and laments. These works were written over hundreds of years, long after the described events, and reached their final edited form only after the return from the Babylonian exile in the sixth century BCE. The historical times in which they were written were quite different from one another – language usage, attitudes, cultural symbols, and conceptions of God all undergo constant change.

Context, Context, Context

When we read the Old Testament or look for verses that will shed light on our lives or offer ethical guidance, we need to keep several things in mind. First, we must understand the context in which a book was written. Even within a book, it is important to separate the strands or streams of tradition we find. As we will see later, a portrayal of God in rather human terms, such as God walking among us or coming down for a face-to-face talk, is a sign that it stems from the Yahwist source (J). A concern for ritual, law, and purity suggests the Priestly source (P), from a later era.

The styles of J and P

> As we travel back in time, we will examine the historical and cultural pressures that produced or influenced the text. Is that context the same as ours?

> We then ask what cultural values dominate the text. For example, Lot offered his two daughters to a mob bent on gang rape in the hope that they would not assault his two angelic guests. As modern people, we are rightfully appalled at his willingness to throw his own children to the wolves, but we also realize that in the ancient Near East, hospitality to strangers was sacred; one was responsible for the lives of one's guests. It 'made sense' in their context, but we should not even consider making it our own practice.

> Finally, we determine what sort of God-image was in the mind of the author when composing the book. God is portrayed as violent and murderous at times, willing to kill thousands for their transgressions. In one account, 'God' struck two men dead for touching the ark of the covenant as it trundled along in a cart that was tipping over. In both instances, ancient concepts of divinity are at work. The divine and transcendent is terrifying and dangerous, and the slightest miscalculation in one's dealings with a deity could be disastrous.

The understanding of God has evolved; people in the 21st century need not and should not carry within them an image of God forged in the 2nd and 1st millennia BCE. In many of these texts, 'God' speaks in the first person – but we should know that most ancient religious texts portrayed their gods in identical ways. There is little difference in rhetoric and style between some of the pages of the Old Testament and inscriptions that archeologists have found in the cultures that surrounded ancient Israel. When we consider the context and the chronological and cultural distance between us and the text, this helps us to draw a more balanced understanding from our reading and reflection.[1]

Themes and Teachings

Although some themes and teachings are consistent throughout the Old Testament, many others changed over time. The Old Testament is in continuous dialogue with itself – one book sometimes responds to another, in support or with a challenge.

After the Israelites entered the Promised Land, they began to do battle against the people there. Joshua declared that all the booty taken during their raids was "devoted to the Lord" – no one was to touch or keep anything at all. One man, Achon, could not resist – he stashed some of the loot after a raid, causing Israel to lose the next battle. In his anger, God told Joshua that "Israel has sinned" – note the focus on the collective rather than focusing on an individual. When Achon was found to be the culprit – through the casting of lots! – he and his entire family were stoned to death and burned.

We are struck by the collective punishment visited on the nation for the actions of one person, as well as by the harshness of the punishment. Jeremiah seems to set that aside in favour of individual responsibility. He is affirmed by Ezekiel in 18:2: "The word of the LORD came to me: What do you mean by repeating this proverb concerning the land of Israel, 'The parents have eaten sour grapes, and the children's teeth are set on edge'? As I live, says the Lord GOD, this proverb shall no more be used by you in Israel. Know that all lives are mine; the life of the parent as well as the life of the child is mine: it is only the person who sins that shall die."

He goes on to explain that the only responsibility one has is to warn the person – after that, the onus is on the sinner. This shows an evolving understanding of human sin and responsibility, as well as how the Old Testament is a form of dialogue.

The Pentateuch, or Books of Moses

The core of the Old Testament is called the Pentateuch, which means "five books" in Greek. The Jewish people refer to this part of the Scriptures as the Torah, which can be translated as "Law" or "teaching." Although Moses was traditionally thought to be the author of the Pentateuch, very few scholars would hold this opinion today. More conservative groups of Jews and Christians, however, still insist on Moses as the author. Scholarship has shown that the books were written centuries later than was first thought, although they often drew on earlier traditions. The five books all anticipate the Promised Land, and the covenant on Mt. Sinai is at its core. They also contain the outline and structure of Israelite society. The thread binding the Pentateuch together is the call of Abraham and the fulfillment of God's promise.

Genesis: The History of the Cosmos, the Creatures of the Earth, and Humans

The story of the Garden of Eden and the eating of the forbidden fruit sets in motion human sin and separation from God. After humans were expelled from the Garden of Eden, human societies were created. The primal murder of Abel releases the poison that affects all human relationships from then on. The first 11 chapters deal with humanity as a whole: it is a rather sorry tale, filled with human failure. Human sin and violence reach such a peak that God regrets creating humans. He wipes out all living things by a catastrophic flood. Only Noah and his family, along with every category of animal, escape in the ark God commanded Noah to build.

God then accepts human weakness; he makes a covenant with humanity and promises that the earth will never be flooded again. Beginning in chapter 12, the focus narrows to one person, Abraham: God calls Abraham and promises to make him the patriarch of a great nation and many descendants. The text describes the trials and tribulations of this very human and dysfunctional family through several generations, along with their interactions with God. Through the adventures of Joseph, son of Jacob, the entire family of Israel migrates to Egypt. Genesis ends with the tribe of Israel living peacefully in Egypt, and Jacob blessing each of his 12 sons, who give their names to the 12 tribes of Israel.

Exodus: Enslavement, Bondage, and Liberation

Exodus begins with the enslavement and bondage of the people of Israel in Egypt, after a change of regime in the land. The Egyptians become nervous because there is a large number of

Israelites and they have a high birth rate. The Pharaoh decides to kill all newborn Israelite males, but brave Hebrew midwives disobey his orders. One child – Moses – is saved from death by being set adrift on the Nile in a small ark; he is adopted by the daughter of Pharaoh and raised in Pharaoh's household. Years later, his killing of an Egyptian overseer who is beating a Hebrew slave causes Moses to flee into exile in the land of Midian. There he marries and settles down to life as a shepherd. But this simple life was not to be; God called to Moses from the burning bush and sent him back into Egypt to confront Pharaoh and demand the release of the Israelites. It is here that God reveals his "name" – which can be translated as "I am who am," "I am that I am," or "I will be who I will be." This means that God is the eternal existent one and resists being named or categorized.

During Moses' confrontation with Pharaoh, God sends 10 terrifying plagues on the Egyptians, with the last plague being the death of all the firstborn children of Egypt. This is the first Passover, where the Destroying Angel passes over Egypt. Several times during this battle of wills, Pharaoh relents and decides to let the Israelites go, but God "hardened his heart," causing him to change his mind. The people are then released, but still have to escape through the sea and avoid Pharaoh's army, which is pursuing them.

As they go forth from Egypt, they are led by a pillar of cloud by day and a pillar of fire by night. During their journey through the Sinai wilderness, the people lose faith and rebel against God, even though God consistently provides for them. There is grumbling and conflict, which sets the pattern for the wilderness journey: faithlessness, rebellion, putting God to the test. This reaches a climax in the notorious golden calf incident. When the people get nervous at Moses' delay on the mountaintop, the Israelites make a calf out of gold and begin to worship it. God is on the verge of wiping them all out, but Moses intercedes. The Levites slaughter many of the guilty. In this book, Moses and the people make a covenant with God at Sinai, and Moses is presented with the tablets containing the Ten Commandments – the Decalogue – and many ritual and cultic regulations. Exodus also describes the tent of meeting – a sort of mobile temple – and the Ark of the Covenant. God descends and dwells in this tent in the form of a cloud, and Moses converses with him face to face, as with a friend.

Leviticus: Dietary and Purity Rules Mingled with Justice

The Book of Leviticus is not the most exciting reading in the world. It contains detailed descriptions of sacrifices, feasts, rituals, many laws and commandments, as well as foods that people are forbidden to eat. It aims to determine one's worthiness and holiness in approaching God. Among these laws are those condemning witches, adulterers, and homosexuals to death. The Holiness Code (chapter 19) is contained within all of the ritual prescriptions: this code commands the Israelites to treat strangers and the people of the land well, to care for the poor and weak, and to love their neighbour as themselves. Jesus later quotes this commandment in the New Testament.

Numbers: Census, Journey, Rebellion, and Wandering

The Book of Numbers parallels the account of the journey through the wilderness recounted in Exodus, but with many variations and more details. A central theme of the book is the faithlessness and failure of the people in the wilderness, despite God's continual supply of food and water. There is a serious challenge to the authority of Moses, even from his own sister, Miriam, and his brother, Aaron. The people refuse to trust God, even doubting the initial reports of the Promised Land brought back by the spies sent ahead of them. They are condemned by God to wander for 40 years in the wilderness, until the generation born in slavery has died off. As they approach their entry into the Promised Land, the King of Moab sends a prophet – Balaam – to curse Israel. He instead gives an oracle and blesses Israel. His star and sceptre oracle in 24:17 became a messianic text; it is later echoed in Revelation 22:16 and Matthew 2:2. Instructions are given for the conquest of Canaan and for the land to be divided among the tribes, along with more laws and regulations. Joshua is named the successor to Moses.

Deuteronomy: The Second Law

The Book of Deuteronomy is portrayed as Moses' reflection on the exodus and the desert journey. The Israelites are poised to enter the Promised Land at long last, and this is Moses' farewell speech, for he will not be permitted to enter. Some Scripture passages (Ezra 3:2; Deuteronomy 1:1; 2 Chronicles 25:4), as well as later tradition, viewed Moses as the author, but Deuteronomy 34:5 also recounts his death. This book contains the *shema* or "Hear, O Israel" (Deuteronomy 6:4-5), the fundamental creed of Israel. It also lays before the people two paths, one to life and the other to death, and bids them choose. If the Israelites follow the path of life closely, they will prosper in the land and receive many blessings; but if they deviate or fall into idolatry, various curses will descend on them. For his part, God promises unfailing fidelity, and vows to bring them back even if they should be scattered throughout the earth. This covenantal theology was extremely long-lasting and influential. In fact, during his temptations in the desert, Jesus counters the temptations of the devil with responses from Deuteronomy that speak of absolute fidelity, exclusivity, and trust in worshipping God.

> Hear, O Israel: The LORD is our God, the LORD alone. You shall love the LORD your God with all your heart, and with all your soul, and with all your might.
> (Deuteronomy 6:4-5)

The Historical Books

The historical books that follow the Pentateuch – Joshua and Judges – are interesting and even exciting reading, but they bring with them a host of interpretative questions and problems. The Book of Joshua is the account of the invasion of the Promised Land under the leadership of Joshua, the designated successor of Moses. God declares, "As I was with Moses, so I will be with you" (1:5), and that appears to be the case. They first send in spies, and win their first battle by defeating the city of Ai (8:18-26). Their spies visit Jericho; they are hidden and helped by Rahab the Harlot, another ancestor of King David and Jesus. The Israelites part the waters of the Jordan in a symbolic re-enactment of the crossing of the Red Sea, then enter the Promised Land. The manna ceases; they circumcise the generation born in the wilderness. After marching around Jericho for seven days blowing trumpets, they give a mighty shout and the walls collapse. The city is placed under the *harem* or ban, meaning destruction of its inhabitants and annihilation of the city. The book ends with the assembled people at the sanctuary of Shechem affirming their covenant with the Lord. Joshua warns them extensively against idolatry, reflecting the theology of Deuteronomy, for the Book of Joshua was written in that tradition.

Key Issues

The Book of Joshua raises questions. In more modern times, Joshua was the ideal Christian warrior. The ruthless, merciless, and bloody conquest and treatment of the inhabitants of the land – supposedly at the command of God – is difficult to reconcile with what we consider fundamental humanity and justice. Even though this type of warfare was the norm at the time, we would expect a higher standard for those who have made a covenant with God. We have seen too many atrocities and instances of ethnic cleansing in the last century, even up to today, that claim some sort of religious sanction. These are often carried out by believing Christians or Jews – such as in the civil war in the former Yugoslavia, the genocide in Rwanda, and the dispossession from the land and mistreatment of the Palestinians. Those responsible would not be rebuked by any passages from Joshua.

The second issue is historical and archeological. Many insist that the Old Testament – especially the historical books – report events accurately. But these are not historical works in our modern understanding of the term. Joshua is theological and ideological history. Many of the events described in this biblical book are not mentioned in any other place – not even in the psalms that recount Israel's history, such as psalms 78, 105, 106, and 136. The second half of the difficulty is the archeological evidence. Excavations at Ai disclose that during the time of the Israelite invasion of Canaan, Ai was unoccupied – empty. Jericho is one of the oldest cities in the world, going back to around 9000 BCE. Even today, one can visit the *tel* or mound of its ruins. There are numerous layers in this mound, and they can be dated with a reasonable degree of accuracy, based on stratification and the types of pottery found in each layer. During the time of the invasion, Jericho, too, was unoccupied – this was one of the many periods in which the city lay deserted. We are left with the claims of the text on the one hand and the archeological evidence on the other, with no real way to reconcile them. More research and excavation may clarify the problem. Meanwhile, we can take care not to make unreasonable claims about the literal truth or the historicity of these texts. And we should not look to them for guidance in waging war or treatment of captive peoples.

A Literary Quilt: A Book of Many Sources

When we read the Old Testament, we are not reading one single book, but many. Even within a particular book, we are reading a number of different traditions and streams, and not all of them agree. That is why it is not desirable to pick a verse out of context to prove a point. Someone else can probably find a verse with an opposing view, even within the same book. The entire Old Testament is a quilt of diverse sources, as is evident in the number of repetitions and contradictions found in the texts. There are two flood stories in Genesis 6–9; two calls of Moses in Exodus 3 and 6; two creation accounts in Genesis 1 and 2–3; two Hagar and Ishmael accounts in Genesis 16 and 21; and two Joseph accounts in Genesis 37. These accounts do not agree in all the details, and no amount of mental juggling will reconcile them. The ancients were not bothered by conflicting or diverse accounts in the same text. In their view, these versions were merely different angles on the truth.

The Old Testament is a weaving together of many different sources and traditions. Not only is it a library of books – each book has a sub-library of sources and traditions. Most of these traditions fall into one of four sources. This is not just some arcane academic point – it is important for us to be aware of them, for each has its own distinct style and theology and contains several sources from different times and places. They are stories within the story. We cannot expect consistency in detail or even in theology in all cases – this is one of the many reasons that the Bible is said to be self-contradictory. But this also makes the Bible so fascinating!

The Four Sources of Biblical Tradition

> **Priestly (P)**: laws and traditions (circa 539 BCE)
> **Yahwist (J)**: viewpoint of the southern kingdom of Judah and its monarchy (circa 950 BCE)
> **Elohist (E)**: the covenant of Moses (8th or 9th century BCE)
> **Deuteronomist (D)**: a final testament of Moses as the Israelites stand poised to enter the Promised Land (mid- to late 7th century BCE)

Source: John J. Collins, *Introduction to the Hebrew Bible*, 3rd ed. (Minneapolis, MN: Fortress, 2018). Note that the dating and sequences for the four sources of biblical tradition are vigorously debated by scholars today.

The Priestly Source

The Priestly source (P) was probably compiled after the exile, around 539 BCE.[2] P is characterized by lists of ancestors, the law collections of Leviticus and Numbers, genealogy lists, and other isolated stories and traditions. It is strongly cultic: it insists on correctness in sacrifice and worship and rigorous observance of the Sabbath. In exile, the compilers of this tradition were concerned with how to keep the covenant with God even when there was no land, temple, or king. God is called "Elohim" and is often described with exalted and majestic speech.

Chapter 1 of Genesis contains P's version of creation. The account is orderly, terse, and elegant. Light, water, land, fish, birds, creatures, and so on come into being at God's spoken command. Finally, humans are created. In a sense, they are not of this earth, for they too are the result of God's command. They are created, male and female simultaneously, in the image and likeness of God, like a statue of the divine. There is no hint that one is superior or subordinate to the other, and in this account, sin and punishment are absent – there is no Fall. In fact, after every act of creation, God declares that "it is good." Interestingly, it appears that in God's original plan, only plants were intended for food: "And to every beast of the earth, and to every bird of the air, and to everything that creeps on the earth, everything that has the breath of life, I have given every green plant for food" (v. 30). This will prevail until after the flood.

Chapters 1 to 11 of Genesis tell a story of origins; this is predominantly from the pen of P. Since this was written during and after the exile in Babylon, it reflects the creation myths of the Babylonians (including those described in the *Enuma Elish*) and other peoples of the Ancient Near East. The author repurposed and refashioned a story in which there was a rebellion in heaven. Matter and spirits have always existed, rather than being created by divine command. There was a war against primeval chaos, represented by the sea monster Tiamat. Light emanating from the gods created the firmament, dry land, and heavenly lights. After creation, the gods rested and celebrated with a banquet. Does this sound familiar? Almost, but not quite. When the author of Genesis finishes with it, God creates by means of a divine spirit or breath (*ruah*) and by speech, but is not himself part of that creation. There is darkness over the deep, and all is formlessness and void. This is followed by the appearance of light, the sky dome, the firmament, heavenly lights, human beings, and God resting on the seventh day. The author has used a pagan creation myth but has purged it of polytheism (many gods) and notions of a cosmic battle. The entire story becomes a testament to the power of God's creative word.

> The *Enuma Elish* was a Babylonian creation myth written on clay tablets. It was discovered in Nineveh during the 19th century. Scholars were quick to note the striking similarities with the Genesis account of creation. The Hebrews borrowed and modified many of these creation stories during the Babylonian exile.

The Yahwist Source

A second source is Yahwist, or J (the name used for God in this source is 'Yahweh'; Jawist is the German term – there is no 'Y' in German). Scholars used to date it to about 950 BCE, during Solomon's reign, but recently there is a tendency to give it a later date. It expresses the viewpoint of the southern kingdom of Judah and its monarchy. God is called "Yahweh" and walks and talks with us, and the language used about God is very earthy. In the Yahwist epic, there are seven steps: the story of human origins, the promise to the patriarchs, the oppression in Egypt, the exodus from Egypt, wandering in the wilderness, the covenant at Sinai, and standing at the edge of the promised land. It forms a continuous story, ending in the Book of Numbers. J is a storyteller – he puts words and speeches in the mouths of significant people. He likes to foreshadow great events, such as in Genesis 15:13-15. There are a number of well-known themes in J: the conflict between brothers, the triumph of the younger over the older, and the barren wife.

A Very Different Creation Story

The Yahwist account of creation in Genesis 2:4–4:26 is different from that of P. The order is different – man is created first, before vegetation and animals, and there was no rain or human tillers. Adam is not actually a person's name. It merely means "of the earth," for God created him from the ground, like a potter fashioning clay, and breathed the spirit of life into him. The Yahwist depiction of God in human terms is evident throughout the story. God created a beautiful garden, filled with lush vegetation and fruit, and set the man in its midst. He was free to help himself to everything except the fruit of the tree at its centre: the tree of the knowledge of good and evil. All the animals are paraded before Adam for him to name. Naming implies mastery over that creature. At this point, God – Yahweh Elohim – realizes that it is not good for the man to be alone. In what might be termed divine cloning, God causes a deep sleep to come over Adam, and then God takes a portion of his rib and fashions a female – Eve. In a sense, the companionship of men and women and marriage itself becomes part of creation, as in verses 24-25: "Therefore a man leaves his father and his mother and clings to his wife, and they become one flesh. And the man and his wife were both naked and were not ashamed."

It is the story of the Garden of Eden that people are most familiar with, and that has had more of an impact on people throughout the centuries. Much theology – both good and bad – is based on this story. The tree in the midst of the garden bestows wisdom, which is the knowledge of good and evil. It is a powerful symbol, for humans have always desired to know and to have the power that wisdom brings. Enter the villain – the serpent – who is, according to the text, clever and cunning. Nothing in the text indicates that this was the devil – indeed, the devil was not part of Israelite tradition at this point. Identification with the devil is a much later tradition. Although later traditions describe the forbidden fruit as an apple, this is not stated anywhere in the text.

As the serpent attempts to convince Eve to eat the forbidden fruit, she demurs, reminding him that God warned them that eating it would bring about their deaths. The serpent scornfully denies this, claiming that God feels threatened – God knows that when they eat the fruit, they will become as gods, knowing good and evil. This is the most insidious part of the story – mistrust is introduced into the relationship between God and humans. God cannot be trusted; God is jealous of his prerogatives. The rupture occurs when the fruit is eaten – the man and woman are suddenly aware that they are naked, and they feel shame. This is the fruit of disobedience: self-awareness, self-assertion, loss of innocence. (Note that this has nothing at all to do with sex.)

They hid from God as he walked in the coolness of the evening – again, the Yahwist depicts God with human characteristics. The punishments were not far behind God's discovery of their disobedience. The serpent gets to crawl forever in the dust and be stepped on. The man will labour and sweat in the fields with minimal results, and the woman will bear children in pain and be dominated by her husband.

This is a teaching story, one of many that circulated in the ancient world. It is not a literal, scientific account of human origins. It is likely that there was no Garden of Eden or Adam and Eve – they are powerful symbols of humanity and its weaknesses. The story explains the origins of the human condition – suffering and mortality – and lays the blame squarely on the human doorstep. The message is clear: God's creation is good; evil and suffering flow from human disobedience and sin. Human sin was not part of the divine plan.

St. Augustine and the doctrine of original sin

A thousand years later, St. Augustine and others would use this text to hammer out a doctrine of original sin, which is still with us today. Augustine held that original sin was guilt passed down almost genetically from generation to generation. That was why baptism was deemed to be so important for infants, for without it they could not enter into heaven. Non-Christian and non-Western peoples were likewise lost without baptism, for original sin barred a person from entering God's presence.

One need only read the morning newspaper to be convinced that original sin is a reality – as cynics have said, it is the only doctrine for which we have empirical proof. But this doctrine cannot be based on a literal interpretation of Genesis 2. Children do not come into this world doomed because someone ate a piece of forbidden fruit millennia ago. Our programmed weakness and tendency to sin is the cumulative effect of bad human choices and deliberate flouting of divine law.

It is not inherited or learned guilt, but negativity and selfishness passed down by example, values, and teaching to the next generation. They are not born racists, bigots, criminals, and oppressors; they are formed that way.

Other negative aspects to this story are still with us. Eve – and all women after her – were branded with the label of temptress. According to this view, Eve was the one who led Adam astray. This led to a negative view of women that lasts to our own day and has been instrumental in the oppression and devaluing of women for centuries.

In fact, neither Adam nor Eve is willing to take responsibility – each points to someone else. The whole issue of being aware of nakedness and shame speaks of coming to self-awareness as creatures separate from God. And this is where fear enters the picture – humans are afraid of being in God's presence and hide from him, and thus it has been ever since. They are banished from the garden, more as an act of mercy than of punishment. If they eat from the tree of immortality, they will be stuck in this fallen state forever. This banishment is deeply etched into our religious consciousness. We long for the Garden and the presence of God, but it seems so far away.

Two Flood Stories – How Many Pairs of Animals?

In the Yahwist's account of the flood, God asks Noah to take seven males and seven females of each type of animal. The water floods the earth for 40 days and nights. In P's account, however, there are only two of each gender and species. The waters flood the earth for 150 days. Which account is 'true'? Probably neither! They are not intended to convey factual historical information, and they represent two different traditions. The ancients were not the least bit perturbed about having contradictory details in the same document – they were more concerned with meaning than facts.

The Elohist Source

A third source is the Elohist, or E. It was written in the northern kingdom of Israel after the death of Solomon, and stresses the covenant of Moses over kingship. It uses spiritualized language in talking about God. After the fall of the northern kingdom to the Assyrians in 722 BCE, J and E were combined by various redactors, or editors. God is called "Elohim" and often speaks in dreams. The fear of the Lord and prophetic warnings are stressed. Interestingly, the mountain where the covenant was given is called Horeb rather than Sinai.

The Deuteronomist Source

A latecomer to the different streams within the Old Testament was one that scholars call D, for Deuteronomist. The Book of Deuteronomy was 'discovered' during temple renovations in 622 BCE, during a period of reforms under the two 'good' kings – Hezekiah and Josiah. This discovery helped to initiate a reform movement of priests, Levites, and prophets to counteract idolatry and the flouting of God's laws throughout Judea. The book is a final testament of Moses as the Israelites stand poised to enter the Promised Land. It is filled with sermons and laws that stress obedience and faithfulness to the covenant. Only by this covenant fidelity will the people receive blessings and dwell in peace in the land. The book is filled with images of warfare and stereotypical phrases. Long speeches stress God's deeds on behalf of Israel. It is very moralistic. D addresses God as "Yahweh." The Deuteronomists reinterpreted Israel's history; we find their fingerprints from Deuteronomy through 2 Kings. According to this ideology, all of Israel's woes stemmed from their sins and lack of fidelity to God. In their account of the kings of Israel, there is usually a set phrase: "And he did what was evil in the sight of the LORD..." – usually tolerating or indulging in idolatry on a large scale.

Divinely Sanctioned Violence

As spiritually fruitful as Deuteronomy is, it also contains a couple of lethal texts. When it was written, idolatry of the gods of surrounding nations was the major problem. The Deuteronomists were convinced that Israelite tolerance for idolatry and for the religions of the peoples of the land had brought the nation low. Therefore, the new edition of the Law – Deuteronomy – stressed the divine command to wipe out all temptations to worship other gods. This includes both the objects of worship and the people of the land. In the eyes of the Deuteronomists, if Israel had done this from the start, they would not be in such a bad situation. The text, a perfect description of ethnic cleansing that is familiar from our own times, should be disturbing:

When the Lord your God brings you into the land that you are about to enter and occupy, and he clears away many nations before you … seven nations mightier and more numerous than you – and when the Lord your God gives them over to you and you defeat them, then you must utterly destroy them. Make no covenant with them and show them no mercy. Do not intermarry with them, giving your daughters to their sons or taking their daughters for your sons, for that would turn away your children from following me, to serve other gods. Then the anger of the Lord would be kindled against you, and he would destroy you quickly. But this is how you must deal with them: break down their altars, smash their pillars, hew down their sacred poles, and burn their idols with fire. For you are a people holy to the Lord your God; the Lord your God has chosen you out of all the peoples on earth to be his people, his treasured possession. (Deuteronomy 7:1-6)

The early pilgrims in the New World drew a direct line from the Canaanites in the Old Testament, citing that God had commanded the Israelites to annihilate the Indigenous peoples in their midst. It was used, very consciously and deliberately, as justification for the slaughter of these peoples and the expropriation of their land.[3]

The biblical characters represent human types, tendencies, attitudes, and behavioural patterns. They are not necessarily to be emulated in every case. They can be examples of actions and attitudes to avoid. For instance, in 2 Kings 2:23-24, the prophet Elisha cursed a group of kids in the name of God because they had teased him for being bald. As a result, a bear came out of the forest and mauled and killed 42 of them. Elisha was a prophet of God, but it is difficult to reconcile this act with that status.

Elijah engaged 450 prophets of the pagan god Baal on Mount Carmel (1 Kings 18:20-40) in a contest to determine the true god – Yahweh or Baal. Each would call on their god to ignite the fire of sacrifice with flame. Despite the self-flagellations, prayers, and dances of the prophets of Baal, their sacrifice remained on the altar untouched by flame. Elijah's prayer was answered; the roaring flame from above consumed the sacrifice, the altar, and everything around it. Elijah completed his victory by killing all the prophets of Baal. This was presented as a great religious act and expression of zeal for the Lord; in the centuries that followed, some people appealed to this story as justification for purging the land of idolatry or heresy.

When 'toxic texts' are read without historical and contextual awareness, they can be lethal. For instance, Exodus 15:3 establishes the dominant image for God for centuries: "The LORD is a warrior; the LORD is his name." This is a root text for many of the violent depictions of God and justifications for holy wars. We do not find the God of Isaiah in this passage, or the God of the Sermon on the Mount. It represents a view of divinity common to the peoples of the Ancient Near East. The god of a people protected them from harm and defeated their enemies on the battlefield – that is just what gods do. A god that could not or would not make them victorious in battle would not inspire awe, respect, or loyalty; the people would be shopping around for a new god. The fact that people viewed divinity in this way in the second or third millennium BCE should not be surprising, shocking, or problematic. It becomes all those things, however, when people insist on the same model of divinity in the 21st century.

> When 'toxic texts' are read without historical and contextual awareness, they can be lethal.

After their narrow escape from the Egyptians and the demise of the pursuing army, the Israelites gaze upon the dead Egyptians washed up along the shore. They break into poetry and praise, and Miriam, the sister of Moses, expresses it in song: she "took a tambourine in her hand; and all the women went out after her with tambourines and with dancing. And Miriam sang to them: 'Sing to the Lord, for he has triumphed gloriously; horse and rider he has thrown into the sea'" (Exodus 15:20-21).

We might ask if it is appropriate to dance and sing in a field of corpses; many rabbis later had similar thoughts. In the Talmud (Megillah 10b and Sanhedrin 39b), God silenced his angels when they began to sing at the death of the Egyptians. His angry rebuke was right on target: "How dare you sing for joy when My creatures are dying!" This is a fine example of midrash – arriving at a deeper understanding of the truth by retelling the story in a different way.

> Jewish tradition held that the Pentateuch did not contain the Law of God in its entirety. Oral law existed before written law and was equally inspired. The Talmud – derived from the word meaning "to study" – is a collection of oral law and commentary that serves as a supplement to the Old Testament.

Likewise, in 1 Samuel 15:3, 'God' commands Saul: "Now go and attack Amalek, and utterly destroy all that they have; do not spare them, but kill both man and woman, child and infant, ox and sheep, camel and donkey." This was supposedly revenge for the Amalekites' refusal to give aid to the Israelites on their way to the Promised Land.

We are all familiar with the notorious Psalm 37, in which a poignant lament for a lost homeland ends with a fervent prayer that someone smash the heads of their oppressors' children against a rock. From a human point of view, the verse is understandable. The exiles had just seen their city and temple destroyed and their own children subjected to such barbaric and cruel treatment. Now they were helpless prisoners, and they longed and prayed for their tormentors and captors to receive like treatment. It is the cry of an oppressed people, a cry of desperation and despair.

Apparent divinely sanctioned violence in these and similar passages is dangerous. When human prejudices and fears meet these texts, a rather dark reaction can be triggered. Making absolute truth claims based upon texts, demanding blind obedience, using them to reinforce group identity, or trying to predict or provoke the end times are all activities guaranteed to create twisted forms of religion.[4] Sometimes passages are erroneously used to bolster injustice, exclusion, prejudice, resentment, or outrage. Just look at the comments section of internet sites that claim to be religious, or read the letters to the editor of some Catholic newspapers. Unfortunately, these negative interpretations sometimes find their way into sermons and homilies. Bad exegesis (explanation of Scripture) equals bad theology, and bad theology usually means that someone suffers as a result.

The Prophets: Conscience of the Nation

These same Scriptures command us to love the Lord our God with all our heart, mind, soul, and strength – and our neighbour as ourselves. Repeatedly and consistently, the Old Testament insists on treating widows, orphans, the poor, and aliens justly. We are continually exhorted to practise kindness and mercy, and to exercise the Golden Rule. These demands are closely connected with Israel's prophets.

The prophetic tradition in ancient Israel is vivid and rich. The prophecies are filled with passion, imagery, and violence. Most of these books are loose collections of oracles given at various times and collected over time, often by the followers of the prophet. The prophecies are written in vivid poetry and are well seasoned with proverbs, laments, hymns, speeches, and prayers. They are often filled with legal-like accusations and charges hurled at the nation and its establishment.

It is from many of the prophetic passages that the Old Testament gets its reputation of being about blood and thunder. The prophets did not predict the future, at least in the sense that we understand prediction. They represented the conscience of the nation and could be described as those who admonished the people and roused their conscience or ethical sensibilities. Their preaching was a wake-up call – smarten up or you will suffer the consequences! Was this punishment from God? It is often portrayed that way, but the disasters the Israelites suffered were most often the natural consequences of bad choices and worse policies. They believed that God shielded them from the predators that surrounded them. When God had finally run out of patience, this shield was withdrawn, and they suffered accordingly. The terrifying prophetic images of slaughter and destruction were based on experience. The ancient lands of the Bible were brutal: the sacking of cities, mass rape and pillage, and the slaughter or enslavement of people were all too familiar. The prophetic message was clear: this is what can and probably will happen to you if you continue on your present course.

Prophets did not focus on ritual or liturgical shortcomings; in fact, there is some contempt for ritual and worship when it is not accompanied by what we would call social justice. The prophets rail against false religiosity and cold consciences. Ancient Israel was the commonwealth of God, with many laws that protected the poor, vulnerable, and marginalized. How much care was being taken to protect the weak and vulnerable and carry out just economic practices determined the nation's spiritual health. These verses are typical of the prophets' calls:

He has told you, O mortal, what is good; and what does the LORD require of you but to do justice, and to love kindness, and to walk humbly with your God? (Micah 6:8)

Hear the word of the LORD, you rulers of Sodom! Listen to the teaching of our God, you people of Gomorrah! What to me is the multitude of your sacrifices? says the Lord; I have had enough of burnt offerings of rams and the fat of fed beasts; I do not delight in the blood of bulls, or of lambs, or of goats.

When you come to appear before me, who asked this from your hand? Trample my courts no more; bringing offerings is futile; incense is an abomination to me.

New moon and sabbath and calling of convocation – I cannot endure solemn assemblies with iniquity. Your new moons and your appointed festivals my soul hates; they have become a burden to me, I am weary of bearing them. When you stretch out your hands, I will hide my eyes from you; even though you make many prayers, I will not listen; your hands are full of blood. Wash yourselves; make yourselves clean; remove the evil of your doings from before my eyes; cease to do evil, learn to do good; seek justice, rescue the oppressed, defend the orphan, plead for the widow. (Isaiah 1:10-17)

I hate, I despise your festivals, and I take no delight in your solemn assemblies. Even though you offer me your burnt offerings and grain offerings, I will not accept them; and the offerings of well-being of your fatted animals I will not look upon. Take away from me the noise of your songs; I will not listen to the melody of your harps. But let justice roll down like waters, and righteousness like an ever-flowing stream. (Amos 5:21-24)

They were not looking into the far future, nor were they prophesying about the Messiah or about Christ. They spoke to the conditions and needs of their times. They rose in prominence during periods of great danger and crisis. The mid-eighth century BCE to the early seventh century BCE (roughly 750–610 BCE) was a time of great threat from the superpower of the time, the empire of the Assyrians. Their state could justly be called a killing machine, for as they ground up and subjugated nation after nation, they treated the defeated peoples with great brutality. Not only that, they were proud of it – stone carvings still exist that show the Assyrian kings having captives beheaded, blinded, and flayed alive. These images sent a powerful message – small wonder that tiny Israel was so frightened.

The first group of prophets, whom scholars call the Twelve Minor Prophets ("minor" because of the length of their works), flourished during this time: Zephaniah, Nahum, Habakkuk, Hosea, Amos, Micah, Haggai, Zechariah, Obadiah, Malachi, Joel, and Jonah. All but Haggai, Malachi, Joel, and Jonah were from the northern kingdom of Israel. The northern prophets knew that this kingdom was first on the Assyrian chopping block. In their passionate preaching, they denounced social and economic injustice, the crushing of the poor, and, as always, idolatry. Some of them used metaphors in their preaching. Hosea claimed that God commanded him to marry a woman guilty of serial infidelities. Throughout his prophecy, he used this as a metaphor for Israel: she was a "whore," just like his wife. But as he continually forgave her and took her back, so God would forgive Israel. As with most of the prophets, their warnings were unheeded, and the Assyrian juggernaut crushed the northern kingdom of Israel in 722 BCE, causing the end of its existence.

> The prophets were not looking into the far future, nor were they prophesying about the Messiah or about Christ. They spoke to the conditions and needs of their times. They rose in prominence during periods of great danger and crisis.

Jeremiah – The Reluctant and Unsuccessful Prophet

One of the most interesting prophets was Jeremiah. He might be called a reluctant prophet – he objected to God's call at the beginning, and several times during his long ministry he threatened to quit. Jeremiah was a man of great inner turmoil and self-doubt. He preached during a tumultuous time, 627–586 BCE: the period of Assyria's waning power and eventual defeat, and the rise of the Babylonians, who soon set their sights on Jerusalem. Jeremiah's message was not what people wanted to hear: the Babylonians would defeat Jerusalem, and it was God's will. They should surrender and serve the Babylonians. The false court prophets surrounding the king counselled resistance, and constantly defamed Jeremiah. There were attempts on his life, and he was imprisoned more than once. His painful prophetic ministry was not successful – what had begun in hope during the reforms of kings Hezekiah and Josiah ended with the destruction of Jerusalem and the temple, and the exile of the people in Babylon. Even towards the end, Jeremiah purchased a plot of land as a symbolic sign of hope in the future. The prophets always left us with a glimmer of hope. But an even grander glimmer of hope was expressed in his prophecy of the new covenant:

> The days are surely coming, says the LORD, when I will make a new covenant with the house of Israel and the house of Judah. It will not be like the covenant that I made with their ancestors when I took them by the hand to bring them out of the land of Egypt – a covenant that they broke, though I was their husband, says the Lord. But this is the covenant that I will make

2. The Old Testament: A Rich and Diverse Library

with the house of Israel after those days, says the Lord:
I will put my law within them, and I will write it on
their hearts; and I will be their God, and they shall be
my people. No longer shall they teach one another, or
say to each other, "Know the Lord," for they shall all
know me, from the least of them to the greatest, says
the Lord; for I will forgive their iniquity, and remember
their sin no more. (Jeremiah 31:31-34)

We should not be too quick to Christianize this passage,
even though some New Testament authors applied it to the
new covenant inaugurated by Jesus (Hebrews 8:8-12; 10:16-
17; 2 Corinthians 3:1-14). It was a prophecy given to the
people of Israel in light of their situation then; in its original
context, it was not referring to Jesus or Christianity. Rather,
it was intended to give them hope of a future, a fresh start,
and a renewal of their communal relationship with God. Its
Christian repurposing was its second life, beyond the original
meaning of the text.

These prophets still live in the spirit of the prophets of our
own time. Amos 5:24's "But let justice roll down like waters,
and righteousness like an ever-flowing stream" has been part
of the repertoire of many contemporary prophets, especially in
the preaching of Martin Luther King. Our takeaway from the
prophets is that God demands from us justice and compassion
towards our fellow human beings, and God will not take no for
an answer. When we continually and obstinately ignore these
demands, we sow the seeds for our own downfall. They remind
us what true worship is and the nature of our relationship
with God. Many of the issues the prophets addressed, such as
economic injustice and the growing gap between the rich and

poor, are still with us today – and are some of the most pressing challenges of our time. Religion must never become a way of soothing our consciences or attempting to buy God off by elaborate displays of worship or personal devotion or asceticism.

> Our takeaway from the prophets is that God demands from us justice and compassion towards our fellow human beings and will not take no for an answer.

Isaiah – The "Fifth Gospel"?

Isaiah is probably the best known of the prophets, and has influenced the New Testament and subsequent Christian theology the most. It has been called the fifth gospel, but in a sense, this is unfair. Many of the things we attribute to the New Testament – universalism, God's presence in the lives of those who do not share our faith, and the primacy of the inner spirit of the law over externals – were present in Isaiah in their own right. The New Testament merely built on what had already been given. The Book of Isaiah was written over a period of 200 years, from about 740 BCE to perhaps 520 BCE. That means it was impossible for Isaiah himself to have written all three sections, although the idea that the entire book was written by one author hangs on stubbornly among some people. The text was written by others in his prophetic tradition and assembled under his name.

Scholars divide Isaiah into first, second, and third Isaiah. First Isaiah was written at various times during the period 740 to 705 BCE, a time of Assyrian threat. It contains several memorable passages, among them the vision of swords being beaten into ploughshares, spears into pruning hooks, and nations no longer training for war (2:3-4). Chapter 6 describes the heavenly journey of Isaiah and his missioning to the nation. The seraphs chanting, "Holy, holy, holy" are echoed in Revelation 4:8, as well as in the Sanctus of the Church's liturgy. It is in chapter 7 that the prophet encourages the beleaguered King Ahaz to be strong and to have faith – the armies that are besieging his people will not overcome them. To bolster his courage, Isaiah offers him a sign – any sign – which Ahaz piously refuses. Isaiah gives him one anyway: "Look, the young woman is with child and shall bear a son, and shall name him Immanuel" (7:14). In the verses that follow, it explicitly states that this was happening in the near future. Otherwise, it would have been senseless. It had nothing to do with a messiah, nor with Jesus. Nevertheless, it became the messianic prooftext for the virgin birth of Jesus and his messianic status.

> **Prooftexting: choosing passages at will to build a case for a particular theological point of view.**

This must be understood as a secondary use of the verse; it will be discussed in chapter 3, on the New Testament. Other passages are appropriated by Christian authors, especially the shoot growing from the stump of Jesse (Isaiah 11). Romans 15:12, 1 Peter 4:14, and Revelation 22:16 all reflect this passage – the yearning for a godly, wise, just, and powerful leader was in all hearts and minds at the time, and these images would be applied to Jesus.

> Many peoples shall come and say, "Come, let us go up to the mountain of the Lord, to the house of the God of Jacob; that he may teach us his ways and that we may walk in his paths." For out of Zion shall go forth instruction, and the word of the Lord from Jerusalem. He shall judge between the nations, and shall arbitrate for many peoples; they shall beat their swords into plowshares, and their spears into pruning hooks; nation shall not lift up sword against nation, neither shall they learn war any more. (Isaiah 2:3-4)

Second Isaiah – chapters 40 to 55 – is sometimes called the Book of Consolation, for it begins with "Comfort, O comfort my people." It was written in exile in the mid-sixth century BCE, and it bears good news for the people: they are going home. Familiar phrases such as "the voice crying in the wilderness" form the opening chapter, and are placed in the mouth of John the Baptist in the Gospels. Cyrus the Persian had defeated the Babylonians; he had a much more tolerant policy towards captive peoples. In fact, chapter 45:1-7 describes Cyrus as the instrument of God and God's messiah or anointed one! That would have been news to Cyrus. This reflected a change in Israel's understanding of God: God was transcendent and worked through nations and kings to accomplish his will. There is a familiar figure in chapters 52 to 53: the nameless and enigmatic individual called the Suffering Servant. We cannot identify the person depicted; in fact, it may be a symbolic figure representing Israel as a whole. This became the lens through which the evangelists viewed the suffering and death of Jesus in the New Testament. Chapter 55 invites all to come to the water and to eat and drink for free. The people cannot hope to pay for salvation, forgiveness, or restoration, so it is offered as a gift, an expression of God's mercy. The messianic covenant once offered to David is now offered to the entire people. There is the insistence that God's ways and thoughts are incomprehensible and far above ours. All is accomplished by his will, which goes forth into the world and does not return to God until all is accomplished.

Third Isaiah was composed after the exile in the early sixth to late fifth centuries BCE and is considered a prophet who came after the exile. The land was devastated; Jerusalem and the temple were in shambles. The people and land were slow to recover, and the optimistic prophecies of Second Isaiah seemed hollow. Third Isaiah is filled with prophecies of a hopeful and happy future: Jerusalem is depicted in radiance and splendour as a beautiful bride and given glorious titles. This was therapy: it told the people that they were still God's beloved and had not been abandoned. It is here that universalism is expressed most fully: all peoples are included in God's grace and mercy. Luke fashioned chapter 61 – in which the prophet reveals that he has been anointed to give good news to the poor, bind up the broken-hearted, proclaim liberty to captives and release to prisoners, and a year of the Lord's favour – into the account of Jesus' debut in the synagogue. Jesus reads this passage there, and declares the prophecy fulfilled in him. Isaiah ends with God's declaration that he is about to create new heavens and a new earth, which is repeated in Revelation 21:1.

It is obvious that Isaiah was one of the major templates used in the early Church's understanding of the redemptive role of Jesus. The New Testament would be much poorer without the influence of Isaiah. At the same time, Isaiah cannot simply be scavenged for Christian prooftexts – its integrity must be respected. It addressed people in the few centuries before Christ and was intended to give them hope and encouragement, as well as reassurance that God was still standing by them.

The Day of the Lord

The "Day of the Lord" – a terrifying day of reckoning – makes its first appearance in some of the Minor Prophets from the post-exilic period. This concept was picked up in the New Testament and connected with the Second Coming (*parousia*) of Jesus.

Malachi was written between 516 and 445 BCE. In 3:1, Malachi records, "I will send my messenger before me" – this is identified with John the Baptist in the New Testament, especially in Matthew 11. It is also linked with the Day of Yahweh (the Lord), a day of punishment. Joel was written around 400 BCE; 3:1-5 promised an outpouring of God's Spirit on all flesh in the last days. This is the basis of the experience of Pentecost in chapter 2 of the Acts of the Apostles – in fact, Peter quotes this passage directly. In an interesting twist, Joel upends Isaiah 2 and Micah 4 by declaring that it is time to beat the ploughshares and pruning hooks back into swords and spears, for holy war is on its way.

Finally, Jonah stems from the mid-fourth century BCE, although it is set in Nineveh centuries before. Nineveh was the capital of Assyria, the heart of darkness for the Israelites. After Jonah preaches doom and destruction to Nineveh within 40 days, the king and the entire people repent in sackcloth, ashes, and fasting. God relents and spares them, much to Jonah's chagrin. As he sulks by the roadside, God chides him and reminds him that the Ninevites matter, too – they are his children, and they didn't know any better. The book explains why prophecy "fails" at times – people have free will and change their ways. It also teaches that even Israel's enemies matter to God. Of course, Jonah's adventures in the belly of the whale are more widely known, especially since this became a symbol in the New Testament for the three days Christ spent in the tomb. But the whale was not the point of the story.

Although not a prophetic book, Ruth is possibly one of the most beloved books in the Old Testament. Ruth is from Moab, and the Moabites were despised by the Israelites. Their women were viewed as temptresses, and cohabitation with them was strictly forbidden (see Numbers 25 and Deuteronomy 23:3). After the death of her Israelite husband (note that the rule had already been broken!), Ruth opts to follow her mother-in-law, Naomi, saying, "Where you go, I will go. Where you lodge, I will lodge; your people will be my people, and your God my God. Where you die, I will die – there will I be buried" (Ruth 1:16-17). Both Naomi and Ruth are widows, and Ruth is a foreigner with little in the way of status or means of support. At the prodding of Naomi, she approaches a landowner named Boaz, who eventually marries her. What is the point of this touching story? Ruth is a good Moabite, loyal and righteous, and she gives birth to a son named Obed, who is the father of Jesse, the father of King David. So the Moabite is a direct ancestor of the great King David, and eventually, of Jesus (Matthew 1:3-6; Luke 3:31-33). Together with Jonah, this story forms part of the tradition in the Old Testament of ongoing conversation – the theme, in this case, being exclusivism versus a more open view. The Ninevites and the Moabites are not to be hated – they are capable of goodness, and some of them have a role to play in Israel's history.

A journey through these prophetic texts discloses several things. They differ in time, life situation, and style. They were not intended to predict events in the distant future, but to deal with the challenges of the time and usually an impending crisis. The prophets hoped that their warnings would rouse people from their spiritual and ethical slumber and amnesia. The bloody and violent images should not terrify us or lead us to think they reflect the nature of God. But they are a reminder that we live in a world created by God, and at the heart of that creation are justice, compassion, and our responsibilities to one another by virtue of the image and likeness we all share.

For Further Reflection

1. How do we explain the two versions of creation in Genesis? Are they mythic or scientific truth? What is the difference between these two types of truth? Is it possible for mythic and scientific truth to coexist?

2. It is often said that the God of the Old Testament is not the God of the New Testament. What is meant by that statement? Reflect on this in light of our present-day understanding of the worldview and cultures of the writers of the Old Testament.

3. What is the Holiness Code as expressed in Leviticus? How does Jesus express this in the New Testament? (See Matthew 22:35-40, Matthew 25:31-46 and Mark 12:28-34.) What does this say to us today? How are we to treat refugees and immigrants? Are we a welcoming community or do we try to protect what we have?

4. What is covenantal theology? How does a covenant differ from a contract? What is God's covenant with the Israelites?

5. Review the two creation stories: one from the Priestly tradition and the other from the Yahwist tradition. How do they differ? What is the purpose of each? How have they influenced theology and attitudes over the centuries – specifically, the doctrine of original sin; attitudes towards women; and humankind's fear of God?

6. How is it possible to explain the presence of violence in the Bible? Does God sanction violence? How should these passages of violence be understood?

7. What did it mean to be a prophet in the Old Testament? What was the message of the prophets? Is this message applicable in our time? What does God demand from us that God demanded from the people of Israel?

3

The New Testament: Many Streams, Many Voices

What exactly are we reading when we open the New Testament? If someone asked us to explain what the New Testament is, how would we respond? Our understanding of these two questions will strongly influence how we read and interpret it.

The New Testament is made up of many different writings created over about a century. Each of the four Gospels was written for a particular community, expressing a unique understanding of the mission and ministry of Jesus. For instance, Matthew is the most Jewish of the Gospels, so Jesus is clearly depicted as the Jewish messiah and there is a great concern for the correct interpretation and observance of the Law. Luke, on the other hand, was written for a largely Gentile audience, so there is minimal concern with the Law.

> Not all the writings of the New Testament are on the same page about everything, but they certainly agree on the essential importance of the life, death, and resurrection of Jesus Christ.

The letters of Paul consist of seven undisputed letters: 1 and 2 Corinthians, Romans, Galatians, Philippians, and 1 Thessalonians. Several others – 2 Thessalonians, Colossians, Ephesians, and 1 and 2 Timothy – were written under his name, but most scholars believe they were written a generation later by some of his followers. All the letters differ from the Gospels in their presentation of Jesus – there is almost no reference to the historical Jesus and his ministry, and only basic references to his teachings.

The remaining letters and the Book of Revelation have distinct spiritualities and views of the proper Christian life. In short, not all the writings of the New Testament are on the same page about everything, but they certainly agree on the essential importance of the life, death, and resurrection of Jesus Christ.

The Gospels Are Not Exact Transcripts of the Words and Deeds of Jesus

How many of the sayings in the New Testament attributed to Jesus were actually spoken by him? This is a difficult question to answer, and it has been at the centre of the controversial historical Jesus research of the past three decades. The Jesus Seminar, using an established set of research tools and procedures, estimated that the figure is around 17%. Other researchers offer a more generous estimate. At the other end of the spectrum are those who believe that every word of Jesus reported in the New Testament is authentic and accurate.

We need not opt for either extreme. Whether Jesus spoke every word attributed to him or not, the words are inspired and inspiring. They reflect the traditions and memories that the early Christian communities had of Jesus and his teachings.

But it is well established by most mainstream New Testament scholars that the four Gospels were written 40 to 60 years or so after the crucifixion of Jesus. Mark was probably written around 70 CE, with Luke and Matthew appearing around 85 CE. The Gospel of John was last; it reached its final form about 90 CE. Again, the dates are informed estimates, for no book in the New Testament contains anything that would date it exactly.

> **None of the four Gospels is an eyewitness account; all rely on both oral and written traditions, some of which could have originated with those who were present. Most of the Gospels were probably not written by the apostles to whom they have been attributed. John was most likely the product of several individuals.**

As scholars have pointed out, the Jesus we see in the Gospels is refracted through the lens of the Easter experience and encounters with the Risen Lord. The authors of the Gospels interpret the words and deeds of Jesus through that experience. For example, John 2:13-22 recounts the so-called cleansing of the temple. Jesus told those questioning his actions that if they destroyed the temple, he would raise it up in three days. Of course, they thought he was referring to the temple itself, but the narrator insists that he was speaking of the temple of his body. This is a reference to his death and resurrection. Verse 22 illuminates the role the Easter event had in the formation of the New Testament: "After he was raised from the dead, his disciples remembered that he had said this; and they believed the scripture and the word that Jesus had spoken." The New Testament is a work of enlightened and inspired memory and interpretation.

In recent years, the results of historical Jesus research have excited a lot of interest – and consternation – in the media. Often the results were couched in sensational and dramatic terms and seemed to cast doubt on the historical reliability of the Gospels. Of course, a radical fringe in this research movement has its own agenda. But there are also reliable and responsible scholars who carefully sift through the material at hand and apply the best historical-critical methods (see chapter 1). The reconstructed image of Jesus that they present is not the "real" Jesus, but merely the Jesus who can be known through historical sources. It is important research, for images of Jesus that are not based in history are dangerous. This example, taken from a German catechism during the Nazi period, illustrates this well:

> Jesus of Nazareth in the Galilee demonstrates in his message and behaviour a spirit which is opposed in every way to that of Judaism. The fight between him and the Jews became so bitter that it led to his crucifixion. So Jesus cannot have been a Jew. Until today the Jews persecute Jesus and all who follow him with irreconcilable hatred. By contrast, Aryans in particular can find answers in him to their ultimate questions. So he became the saviour of Germans.[1]

This is shocking to those not used to a jack-booted, swastika-wearing Jesus. During this period, many of the churches in Germany claimed – sometimes backed by scholars who had anesthetized their consciences – that Jesus was not a Jew, and not a drop of Jewish blood flowed in his veins. This is, of course, nonsense on many levels – historical, theological, and moral, for a start. This makes it truly clear that a healthy Christology needs to be based on sound biblical and historical research. We have nothing to fear from sound historical Jesus research.

> Christology is the branch of theology that studies the person, nature, and role of Jesus Christ. In the early Church, it dealt with the divine and human natures of Christ and their relationship to each other. The focus in recent years has been the manner in which Christ relates to humanity and his role in our salvation.

The Gospels reflect two periods in time: the earthly life of Jesus, and the time in which they were written, a generation or more later. For example, John 9 relates the story of the healing of the man born blind. Jesus certainly gave sight to the blind during his earthly life, and this story is probably based on one of those incidents. But the way it is presented as a story in its final written form reflects a much later time – 90 to 100 CE. When the parents of the blind man were interrogated by the authorities, they were afraid to answer. The narrator explains that it had been decreed that anyone confessing Jesus as the Messiah would be expelled from the synagogue – in effect, excommunicated. There is no evidence that this was the case during the lifetime of Jesus. There was, however, considerable tension between Jesus, followers and the synagogue towards the end of the first century, and that is likely the source of this twist on the healing story.

The Gospels: Four Unique Stories of Jesus

As mentioned above, each of the Gospels is a unique telling of the story of Jesus, complete with its own theology and interpretation of events. Even when they all relate the same incident, each does it in a particular way, often modifying the dialogue and details.

The Passion Narratives

This is evident in the passion narratives and the account of the resurrection. But what are the passion narratives? The traditional outlook – and the one that persists in the minds of many – is that everything happened exactly as narrated in the Gospels. A close examination, however, shows that all four accounts cannot be literally true (remember the distinction between literal truth and theological truth).

At the other end of the spectrum is extreme skepticism about the historicity of the narrative. According to some scholars, Jesus was killed on sight by military officials and his body left to the dogs. In this view, the passion narratives are fictional, seasoned with Scripture quotes to "historicize prophecy." Neither of these extremes is satisfactory – as is often the case, the truth lies somewhere in between. There is a basic framework of historical fact: Jesus was arrested, tried, sentenced to death, and executed on the cross. But overlaid on this framework are Scripture quotes, dialogue, and details that give theological interpretations of historical facts. The docudrama is a reasonable modern analogy. It relates historical events and persons, but in the telling of the story, creates dialogue and details to flesh out the story.

Each of the four evangelists has a particular slant in telling the story of Jesus' death. The Gospel accounts converge in the essential details: Jesus was condemned, nailed to the cross between two thieves, died, and then taken down and placed in a tomb. The fine details differ considerably. In Mark and Matthew, Jesus gave a loud cry and breathed his last. The centurion at the foot of the cross exclaims, "Truly this man was God's son!" Jesus is alone in his final moments; all his disciples have fled. Matthew also recounts an earthquake at the time of Jesus' death, the opening of the tombs of holy people, and their appearance in the city. Luke differs significantly: before his death, Jesus prays that God forgive those who have killed him. The cry of Jesus was a statement of trust and self-giving: "Father, into your hands I commend my spirit!" The centurion exclaims, "Certainly this man was innocent!" Immediately before his death, and only in Luke, there is an extended dialogue between Jesus and the two thieves. When we move to the Gospel of John, everything changes. The centurion disappears altogether, replaced by the mother of Jesus, the women with her, and the Beloved Disciple. Jesus places Mary into the care of the Beloved Disciple, and the disciple is given to Mary as her son. When Jesus dies, he exclaims, "It is finished," and gives up his spirit. Only John contains the account of the piercing of the side of Jesus.

There are sound theological reasons for these differences. Mark and Matthew are concerned with the status of Jesus as God's son and the savagery of his crucifixion. Luke stresses forgiveness and the innocence of Jesus. John always portrays Jesus as being in complete command, and as having accomplished his mission from the Father down to the smallest detail. There are no earthquakes or open tombs, as in Matthew.

The Resurrection Accounts

Mark's account, the earliest, is spare in details. The women go to the tomb on the first day of the week to anoint the body of Jesus. They wonder who will roll away the huge stone so they can enter the tomb. When they arrive, they are surprised to find the stone already rolled away, and a young man dressed in white sitting there. The man assures them that Jesus is not there; he is risen – and they are to all meet him in Galilee. The oldest hand-copied manuscripts that we have of Mark end at verse 8 – the women ran away and told no one, for they were afraid. As usual, Matthew is dramatic: there is again an earthquake, and an angel of the Lord descends from heaven and rolls back the stone. The angel's appearance is dazzling, like lightning. He then relates the same message as Mark, but as the women run away, they bump into Jesus, who greets and reassures them, and tells them to go to Galilee. As with Mark, in Luke's account the stone is already rolled away and the body missing. Two men in dazzling clothes appear beside them. Instead of telling them to go to Galilee, they remind the disciples of what Jesus had told them while they were in Galilee: the Son of Man must be handed over to sinners, crucified, and rise again on the third day – a set piece declaration in Luke's Gospel. The women then run to tell the others. John's Gospel is even more divergent: Jesus was anointed by Joseph of Arimathea and Nicodemus before being placed in the tomb. Mary Magdalene goes to the tomb alone and finds it empty. No angels; no young men; no message. When she tells the others, Peter and the Beloved Disciple race to the tomb; they see that it is empty, with the face covering rolled up and placed to one side. They then return home, leaving Mary Magdalene to weep alone outside the tomb, where she encounters the risen Jesus.

Each of these four accounts is true – theologically. All four have a vital message, and each of the four traditions needs to be respected. It is not helpful to try to reconcile the divergent accounts and explain away differences. Remember: in that time, the story was the vehicle of theology and teaching. The four narratives do not represent modern historical method or reportage, and there is no reason why they should.

The Sad and Disgraceful Record of Christian Persecution of the Jewish People

In the year 2000, Pope John Paul II made a historic journey to Jerusalem. After meeting with various leaders, he visited the Western Wall, and as thousands do each day, he deposited a prayer between the stones. It read:

> God of our fathers,
> you chose Abraham and his descendants
> to bring Your name to the nations:
> we are deeply saddened
> by the behaviour of those
> who in the course of history
> have caused these children of Yours to suffer
> and asking Your forgiveness
> we wish to commit ourselves
> to genuine brotherhood
> with the people of the Covenant.

Why did he make this prayer? Why did Christians do so much harm to the Jewish people? It was not until the Second Vatican Council that the Church formally repudiated the collective guilt that had fuelled so much anti-Semitic hatred and violence through the centuries. In 1965, the Declaration on the Relation of the Church to Non-Christian Religions, *Nostra Aetate*, stated, "According to the apostle Paul, the Jews, because of their ancestors, still remain very dear to God, whose gifts and calling are irrevocable."[2] During a visit to a synagogue in Mainz, Germany, in 1980, Pope John Paul II spoke of "The encounter between the people of God of the Old Covenant, which has never been abrogated by God, and that of the New Covenant is also an internal dialogue in our Church, similar to that between the first and second part of its Bible."[3]

Nostra Aetate – "in our time" – was one of the decrees of the Second Vatican Council (1962–65). It dealt with non-Christian religions, highlighting the truth and goodness found in each of them. It also repudiated the mistaken notion that the Jewish people were responsible – both then and now – for the death of Jesus.

Anti-Jewish theology and attitudes stemmed not only from misreading the Bible, but also from miswriting it. A tragic flaw running through the pages of the New Testament has caused much persecution, death, and misery through the centuries. This flaw is called theological anti-Semitism; its cousin, supersessionism, is also harmful.

Supersessionism: the idea that Christianity supersedes Judaism and renders it obsolete.

Several New Testament passages disparage and denigrate the Jewish people. Written in the tumultuous first century as the Christian movement and Judaism were going through their acrimonious divorce, such passages reflect bigotry, triumphalism, and the demonization of opponents. That this ideology is still with us is demonstrated by Mary Boys in her sobering work *Has God Only One Blessing?* The following statements mirror a negative view of Judaism and its people that have been demolished by scholarship and dialogue. Unfortunately, they still persist in the minds of many:

> The God of the Old Testament is a God of wrath. The God of the New Testament is a God of love.

> The Jews rejected Jesus as their messiah because they were waiting for a royal, glorious messiah and could not recognize Jesus as a suffering messiah.

> The self-righteous and hypocritical Pharisees show how legalistic Judaism had become by Jesus' day.

> The Jews were unfaithful to their covenant with God, so their covenant has ended. Christians are now the people of God.[4]

From 66 to 73 CE, the Jewish nation rose in revolt against their Roman occupiers. At first, they seemed to have the upper hand, and the Romans were retreating. But Rome was patient. A large military force, commanded by Vespasian and his son Titus, landed and began campaigning throughout Galilee. One by one, the rebel strongholds fell. It was during one of these campaigns that Josephus the historian was captured. Throughout the war, Josephus witnessed most of the catastrophic events that he described in his *Jewish Wars*; this account is practically the only source we have for the war and its aftermath. Today, one can see the tragedy of the war carved on the Arch of Titus in Rome. Jewish captives with ropes around their necks pull carts full of treasure through the streets for Vespasian's victory parade, including the huge menorah or candlestick from the temple. We still feel the shockwaves from those events today, for there is a direct line from the dispersal of the Jews throughout the world and the centuries of persecution and violence, to the Holocaust, to the re-establishment of the State of Israel in 1948 and tensions in the Middle East.

The Jewish war and its aftermath are particularly important for understanding the New Testament. It was a catastrophe and trauma for the Jewish people. To help us understand its impact, we can look to 9/11 in our own time, but the temple's loss was even greater, since it was the house of God and the heart of the nation.

Mark, Matthew, and Luke are called the Synoptic Gospels. Synoptic means "with one view": these three Gospels have so much in common that it is obvious there is a literary relationship between them. Mark was written first; years later, Matthew and Luke both copy Mark independently and add material of their own, as well as editorial changes. For instance, Mark 13 describes the destruction of the Temple and the final apocalyptic tribulations. We find parallel accounts in Matthew 24 and Luke 21. Both these latter Gospels copy Mark nearly word for word in places, but make some major editorial changes.

The Catastrophe: The Destruction of the Temple

The destruction of the temple casts a large shadow over all four Gospels. Mark 13 and its parallels in Matthew 24 and Luke 21 describe the event and the signs of the end times that follow soon afterward. But it is portrayed as a prophecy from the mouth of Jesus. Jesus – and any astute observer in the first century – might have predicted disaster if the people continued to provoke and defy the Romans. The Gospel accounts, however, are very precise – they describe Jerusalem surrounded by armies and trampled by Gentiles. It is a description of events that have already taken place. The after-the-event prophecy gave theological meaning to all that had transpired. The authors of the Gospels (the evangelists) lay the blame for the disaster on the Jews. In their minds, this was God's retribution for rejecting and crucifying Jesus. This view is reflected in several sayings attributed to Jesus. For example, in Mark, the evangelist rewrote the song of the vineyard from Isaiah 5, addressed many centuries before to the people of Israel:

> Then he began to speak to them in parables. "A man planted a vineyard, put a fence around it, dug a pit for the wine press, and built a watchtower; then he leased it to tenants and went to another country. When the season came, he sent a slave to the tenants to collect from them his share of the produce of the vineyard. But they seized him, and beat him, and sent him away empty-handed. And again he sent another slave to them; this one they beat over the head and insulted. Then he sent another, and that one they killed. And so it was with many others; some they beat, and others they killed. He had still one other, a beloved son. Finally he sent him to them, saying, 'They will respect my son.' But those tenants said to one another, 'This is the heir; come, let us kill him, and the inheritance will be ours.' So they seized him, killed him, and threw him out of the vineyard. What then will the owner of the vineyard do? He will come and destroy the tenants and give the vineyard to others. Have you not read this scripture:

3. The New Testament: Many Streams, Many Voices

'The stone that the builders rejected has become the cornerstone;
this was the Lord's doing, and it is amazing in our eyes'?"

When they realized that he had told this parable against them, they wanted to arrest him, but they feared the crowd. So they left him and went away. (Mark 12:1-12)

The parable of the wicked tenants is a particularly potent weapon in the arsenal of the evangelists. It clearly refers to the Jews and the belief that they had killed the prophets and had not given God his due, thereby invalidating the covenant. The reference to the man coming to make an end to them is chilling, for it is an after-the-event prophecy of the destruction of the temple. Matthew's version of this story (21:33-46) is even more to the point, stating that the kingdom of God will be taken away from them and given to those who will produce fruit. The quotation from Psalm 118:22-23 was a key text for Christian self-understanding during this period: God had vindicated the rejected Jesus and made him the foundation of the new covenant and new temple.

The new version focused on Israel's rejection of the prophets and the killing of the owner's son – Jesus. This is a foundational text for what scholars call supersessionism – the belief that the coming of Jesus revoked God's covenant with Israel and rendered Judaism obsolete and superseded. The loss of life and destruction of 70 CE was confirmation, in Matthew's eyes, that the kingdom of God had been taken away from the Jewish people and given to new tenants – the Christian community. Matthew was writing theology for his day and for the pressures that his community faced, but this is not a valid theological response today.

Ironically, some Jews also thought that Jerusalem's destruction was due to their sins – not upholding the law and traditions of Israel zealously enough and allowing a Gentile power to rule them. Human beings tend to assign blame for catastrophes, but it is highly questionable that this can be laid on God's doorstep. It was a tragedy arising from the power politics, social changes, and imperial rule of the first century CE. There is no need to drag God into the picture – humans do quite well in bringing disaster on themselves.

One of the many ways the evangelists drive home their point that the destruction of the temple was divine retribution is reflected in the so-called cleansing of the temple from the Gospel of Mark:

> On the following day, when they came from Bethany, [Jesus] was hungry. Seeing in the distance a fig tree in leaf, he went to see whether perhaps he would find anything on it. When he came to it, he found nothing but leaves, for it was not the season for figs. He said to it, "May no one ever eat fruit from you again." And his disciples heard it.

> Then they came to Jerusalem. And he entered the temple and began to drive out those who were selling and those who were buying in the temple, and he overturned the tables of the money changers and the seats of those who sold doves; and he would not allow anyone to carry anything through the temple. He was teaching and saying, "Is it not written,

'My house shall be called a house of prayer for all
the nations'?
But you have made it a den of robbers."

And when the chief priests and the scribes heard it,
they kept looking for a way to kill him; for they were
afraid of him, because the whole crowd was spellbound
by his teaching. And when evening came, Jesus and
his disciples went out of the city.

In the morning as they passed by, they saw the fig tree
withered away to its roots. Then Peter remembered and
said to him, "Rabbi, look! The fig tree that you cursed
has withered." (Mark 11:12-21)

This is not a cleansing so that sacrifice can go on as before.
If we look at the reference from Jeremiah 7:11, it is obvious that
the den of thieves is a place to which robbers retire after their
crimes. Jeremiah tears a strip off worshippers for practising
injustice, corruption, and infidelity and for using the temple
worship as a way of soothing (or deadening) their conscience.
The fig tree is an image taken from Jeremiah 8:13, in which
God declares, "they shall be overthrown ... no more grapes on
the vine, nor figs on the fig tree; even the leaves are withered."
The fig tree signifies Israel. In this carefully crafted account of
the cursing of the fig tree (resulting in its withering) and of
the cleansing of the temple, there is clear evidence that Mark
intends it as a prophecy – even a solemn curse – against the
temple itself. Again, this need not signify anti-Judaism as such,
for the prophets spoke of it in the Old Testament.

The Pharisees – Heroes or Villains?

The Pharisees do not fare well in the New Testament. The term "Pharisee" has entered our culture as synonymous with hypocrisy and narrow-minded legalism. In fact, the Pharisees were a highly respected lay movement and were not part of the temple hierarchy, which was predominantly Sadducee. Their fundamental belief was that those living in the towns and villages had a right to live according to the law just as the priests in the temple did. It is in Matthew that we find some of the most odious comparisons of the teachings of Jesus with the practices of the Pharisees and other Jews. This was instrumental in creating the cultural image of the hypocritical Pharisee:

> "And whenever you pray, do not be like the hypocrites; for they love to stand and pray in the synagogues and at the street corners, so that they may be seen by others. Truly I tell you, they have received their reward."
> (Matthew 6:5)

In an extended diatribe, Matthew 23:13-32 condemns and vilifies the scribes and Pharisees. They are hypocritical; they love honour and money; they heap burdens on others but do not raise a finger to help them. The same could probably be said about some members of the religious establishment in every religion and in every age. These accusations portray human failings rather than the characteristics of any particular group.

Are these the historical words of Jesus? Probably not. It is likely that Jesus had negative encounters with opponents during his ministry, but a blanket condemnation of an entire group of people is not in keeping with the core of Matthew's

Gospel. In the Sermon on the Mount, Jesus forbade his followers to insult or speak sharply to another, and he urged his followers to love their enemies and pray for them. These verses likely reflect the tension in Matthew's time rather than during the lifetime of Jesus. The observance of the Law was a controversial issue at the time this Gospel was written. There were two rival Jewish groups: one recognized Jesus as the Messiah, while the other did not. The Pharisees probably belonged to the latter group.

Words are dangerous, especially when they are spoken in anger, and most of all when written down, for they take on a life of their own. Harsh words between Jewish followers of Jesus and their Jewish compatriots are understandable in their historical context. Unfortunately, people long after them had no appreciation of the historical context and preferred to think that the Jewish people were cursed forever. A key text in the Gospel of Matthew is from the trial of Jesus:

> So when Pilate saw that he could do nothing, but rather that a riot was beginning, he took some water and washed his hands before the crowd, saying, "I am innocent of this man's blood; see to it yourselves." Then the people as a whole answered, "His blood be on us and on our children!" So he released Barabbas for them; and after flogging Jesus, he handed him over to be crucified. (Matthew 27:24-26)

Words are dangerous, especially when they are spoken in anger, and most of all when they are written down, for they take on a life of their own. Harsh words between Jewish followers of Jesus and their Jewish compatriots are understandable in their historical context. Unfortunately, people long after them had no appreciation of the historical context and preferred to think that the Jewish people were cursed forever.

These words in Matthew 27 were written with the recent destruction of Jerusalem and the temple in mind. In the mind of the evangelist, this divine retribution has already been fulfilled. Tragically, this is the prooftext for the charge of blood guilt that was applied to all the Jewish people from that time forward and that contributed to their immense persecution and suffering. This collective guilt was not formally repudiated until the Second Vatican Council, in the decree *Nostra Aetate*. Matthew takes great pains to exonerate the Romans, and especially Pontius Pilate: with the washing of the hands (found only in Matthew), the blame is placed squarely on the shoulders of the Jews. In reality, the death of Jesus was the result of the machinations of a few in the temple hierarchy and the Roman authorities, and they alone are responsible.

Luke's treatment of the Jewish people is a bit more complex. He divided his two-volume work (Luke and Acts) into three epochs: the time of Israel, represented by the infancy narrative; the time of Jesus, which was the earthly life of Jesus; and the time of the Church, which began at Pentecost and was carried to the ends of the earth.

In the time of Israel, fulfillment is the overriding theme. The story begins in the Temple during prayer, the characters are pious observant Jews, and all the prayers and hymns reflect Jewish themes and piety. Jesus is welcomed as the long-promised messiah and deliverer. When Mary and Joseph bring Jesus to the Temple, Simeon's words of blessing ring out: "a light for revelation to the Gentiles and for glory to your people Israel." This theme of universalism (Luke 2:32) flows from Second Isaiah – the light of revelation to the nations. But beginning in Luke 4:16-30, the universalism sparks the first resistance to Jesus, and is the first indication of a movement towards the Gentiles and away from Israel.

In Luke 24:46-48 and Acts 1:8, the followers of Jesus are charged with a universal mission to carry the proclamation of the word to the ends of the earth. Unfortunately, this outward direction will be at the expense of Israel. In the Acts of the Apostles, Luke's anti-Israel theology begins to unfold. In Peter's speech to the inhabitants of Jerusalem, they are given another chance to accept Jesus, but the accusation is clear: "But you rejected the Holy and Righteous One and asked to have a murderer given to you, and you killed the Author of life, whom God raised from the dead. To this we are witnesses" (Acts 3:14-15).

In Acts 3:17-21, the leaders are excused because of ignorance and given a second chance to accept Jesus, highlighting that they had been given every opportunity. At the stoning of Stephen in Acts 7:51-53, Stephen accuses them:

"You stiff-necked people, uncircumcised in heart and ears, you are forever opposing the Holy Spirit, just as your ancestors used to do. Which of the prophets did your ancestors not persecute? They killed those who foretold the coming of the Righteous One, and now you have become his betrayers and murderers. You are the ones that received the law as ordained by angels, and yet you have not kept it."

Beginning with the stoning of Stephen, opposition to the Christian movement intensifies, and the Church suffers many persecutions, some led by Saul. Throughout the preaching of Paul and his companions, the message is greeted with resistance and hostility.

After Paul makes his appearance, the persecutor-turned-apostle begins his missionary journeys, constantly battling opponents in the synagogues where he preaches and suffering at their hands. After his arrest and arrival in Rome, he preaches to the Jewish community, and when they reject his message, the Acts of the Apostles ends with Paul quoting from Isaiah (a standard New Testament source of anti-Jewish polemical passages), indicating that the Jews were a lost cause:

> So they disagreed with each other; and as they were leaving, Paul made one further statement: "The Holy Spirit was right in saying to your ancestors through the prophet Isaiah,
>
> 'Go to this people and say,
> You will indeed listen, but never understand, and
> you will indeed look, but never perceive.
> For this people's heart has grown dull, and their ears are hard of hearing, and they have shut their eyes; so that they might not look with their eyes, and listen with their ears,
> and understand with their heart and turn – and I would heal them.'
>
> Let it be known to you then that this salvation of God has been sent to the Gentiles; they will listen." (Acts 28:25-28)

In this ending, the Jews are viewed as definitively rejecting Jesus. Luke shows that God was faithful, that the Jews had
many chances, and that all was foretold by Scripture.

The Gospel of John has been viewed as the most anti-
Semitic in tone and rhetoric, or more correctly, anti-Judaic,
since the writers were all Jews themselves. In 1:17, the text
informs us that "the Law comes through Moses, grace and
truth come through Jesus Christ." This introduces a theme of
replacement in the Gospel. With the arrival of Jesus, Judaism
is replaced by Christ and his followers and becomes obsolete.
Throughout the narrative, there is a negative portrayal of "the
Jews." The groups of Jews with whom Jesus argues are "blind"
or prefer to walk in darkness; the temple personnel plot the
murder of Jesus, which culminates in "the Jews" howling for
the blood of Jesus before an ambivalent Pilate.

Whereas the other three Gospels name the opponents of
Jesus according to the group to which they belong (Pharisees,
Sadducees, etc.), John uses one blanket term for all the enemies
of Jesus and those opposed to God: *hoi ioudaioi*, or 'the Jews',
71 times. This makes no sense – Jesus, his family, his disciples,
and everyone in the Gospel are Jews! Nicodemus and Joseph
of Arimathea are said to be followers of Jesus, but secretly, for
"fear of the Jews." Again, this is ludicrous, for they themselves
were Jews. It is a blanket term applied to all opponents of
Jesus, real or imagined. There were a couple of positive references – in 4:22, Jesus tells the Samaritan woman that salvation
comes from the Jews, while in 8:56, Jesus tells the crowd that
Abraham rejoiced and was glad to see this day.

In a carefully choreographed account of Jesus' ministry,
the rituals of the Jews are replaced by the person of Jesus: the
replacement theme is present in the wedding feast at Cana, or

in the proclamations of Jesus in the temple as he states that he is the light of the world and the source of living waters. These are set against the backdrop of the Jewish feast of Tabernacles and feature images from Old Testament prophecies in which living waters gush from the temple in the last days.

Perhaps most damaging, however, is the debate Jesus has with a group of Pharisees and other Jews. They stand on their claim of being Abraham's children. Jesus counters by saying that if that were so, they would recognize the one sent from God, when in fact they are seeking to kill him. They can therefore not be Abraham's children, but can only be the offspring of the devil ("your father [is] the devil" [8:44]).

> "I know that you are descendants of Abraham; yet you look for an opportunity to kill me, because there is no place in you for my word. I declare what I have seen in the Father's presence; as for you, you should do what you have heard from the Father."

> They answered him, "Abraham is our father." Jesus said to them, "If you were Abraham's children, you would be doing what Abraham did, but now you are trying to kill me, a man who has told you the truth that I heard from God. This is not what Abraham did. You are indeed doing what your father does." They said to him, "We are not illegitimate children; we have one father, God himself." Jesus said to them, "If God were your Father, you would love me, for I came from God and now I am here. I did not come on my own, but he sent me. Why do you not understand what I say? It is because you cannot accept my word. You are from

your father the devil, and you choose to do your father's desires. He was a murderer from the beginning and does not stand in the truth, because there is no truth in him." (John 8:37-44)

In other words, they were not behaving as if Abraham were their father, for he was known for his faith. This polemical statement, wrenched from its context, was taken to be a divine judgment of the Jewish people, rather than a sharp rejoinder to a group of opponents. "Your father [is] the devil" has been one of the chief tools in the arsenal of hate rhetoric through the centuries; it was used by an armed and angry man in October 2018 when he murdered 11 Jews at prayer in Tree of Life synagogue in Pittsburgh.

This is the last of the Gospels written – probably around 90 to 100 CE – and in John 9:22, the healing of the man born blind, we have a hint at its context. The parents of the man whom Jesus has restored to sight are questioned by the Pharisees who cast doubt on the healing and the fact that the man was blind from birth. The parents reply that the authorities can question their son themselves, since he is of age, and the narrator adds, "His parents said this because they were afraid of the Jews; for the Jews had already agreed that anyone who confessed Jesus to be the Messiah would be put out of the synagogue" (9:22). This reflects the situation not in the time of Jesus, but in the time in which the Gospel was written. It is a witness to the growing estrangement between Jews of the synagogue and those who followed Jesus. In the period following the destruction of the temple, Jewish scholars and rabbis defined very precisely what it meant to be a Jew. It was no longer possible to be both a Jew and a follower of Jesus.

Throughout Romans 9–11, Paul agonizes over the failure of his fellow Jews to accept Jesus as the Messiah. In 9:3, his pain becomes evident as he cries out, "For I could wish that I myself were accursed and cut off from Christ for the sake of my own people, my kindred according to the flesh." He focuses on Israel and is generous in his praise. Paul highlights Israel's vital role in salvation history and its many accomplishments. He poses rhetorical questions that imply Israel and the Law are of no account, and answers each one with a forceful "By no means!" He was convinced that this unbelief was both temporary and ordained by God. He writes,

> I want you to understand this mystery: a hardening has come upon part of Israel, until the full number of the Gentiles has come in. And so all Israel will be saved; as it is written,

> "Out of Zion will come the Deliverer,
> he will banish ungodliness from Jacob."
> (Romans 11:25-26)

The question must be seen from God's vantage point, not ours. Paul wrote this in expectation of an imminent return of Jesus and the end of history, so it made sense to him. Two thousand years later, it has lost its force as an explanation for Jewish refusal of Jesus. But we should welcome this passage as a realization that in salvation history, all peoples have their role, and it is never possible to say that any group has been rejected by God.

Many people are unaware that the writers of the New Testament were nearly all Jews. "The Scriptures" they referred to were what we call the Old Testament! Here "Old" does not mean outdated or obsolete (as it does today) but venerable and ancient. One of the charges that the Church Fathers were eager to refute is that Christianity was a new religion. To counter this accusation, they went to great pains to link it to the Old Testament and Israel's salvation history, insisting that their faith was old and worthy of respect. Many of the prayers – the Our Father, for instance – are thoroughly Jewish in nature. These are some important principles to keep in mind when reading the New Testament.

The Old and New Testaments: United by the Dynamism of Love

In 2002, the Pontifical Biblical Commission published a document that truly represented a sea change in how we view the Old Testament and its relationship to the Jewish people. In *The Jewish People and Their Sacred Scriptures in the Christian Bible*, the commission laid a new foundation for a Christian understanding of the Old Testament and its role in salvation history, as well as the relationship to the Jewish people. It represented a new direction in interpreting the Old Testament and its application to theology. For instance, the document insists that a Jewish reading of the Old Testament is both possible and defensible. Second, Jewish expectations of a messiah are not in vain – they are not waiting for the train that will never arrive. Jews and Christians are both waiting for the same train. The document states, "The Jewish expectation for the Messiah is not in vain. It can become for us Christians a strong stimulus to maintain alive the eschatological dimension of our faith. We also, like them, live in expectation. The difference lies in the fact that for us He who will come will have the attributes of that Jesus that has already come and is already present and active in us."[5]

Although condemning harsh Christian behaviour and misapplication of the texts, it seems reluctant to admit that there is an inherent anti-Judaism in many of the passages of the New Testament. In doing this, the document points out that nothing was said that the Old Testament prophets would not have said. This is a partial truth, for classical prophecy could be very harsh and even violent in its rhetoric. But the Jews in the Old Testament are never accused of deicide (the murder of God), nor are they ever told that God has abandoned and repudiated them.

The fulfillment of prophecies has always been a contentious issue in Jewish–Christian relations. They are not, as the document states, "photographic anticipation of future events."[6] They had a meaning and role for their contemporaries and helped them understand the events in their time from the viewpoint of God. The fuller meaning lies in the future. For example, Matthew 1:23 quotes Isaiah 7:14, "The virgin shall conceive and bear a son, whom they shall call Emmanuel." This prophecy was given in the eighth century BCE for King Ahaz when Jerusalem was under siege, and it had immediate relevance then. We are cautioned against polemics based on fulfillment of prophecies, for in the past Jews were judged to be willfully ignorant or obstinate for not seeing the "obvious" fulfillment of the Old Testament prophecies in Jesus. The Christian reading of the Old Testament is done in retrospect. It is not that Jews do not see, but the Christian, with the aid of the Spirit, is able to discover an additional hidden meaning in the text. Since Matthew was concerned with anchoring Jesus firmly in the Jewish tradition, his Gospel abounds with "fulfillment" quotations (1:23; 2:6, 15, 17, 23; 4:14). They should be understood as Matthew's community reading backwards to illuminate their experience of the life, death, and resurrection of Jesus.

> One does not hear or read the prophecy and come to faith; one comes to faith and then hears the prophecy.

The following points represent the essence of the new viewpoint described in the document. We should keep them in mind when reading the New Testament, especially passages that seem hostile to Judaism and the Jewish people.

> ⟩ The New Testament recognizes the authority of the Old Testament and bases itself on that authority. "Without the Old Testament the New Testament would be an indecipherable book, a plant deprived of its roots and destined to dry out." (IV.A.84)

> ⟩ The New Testament must be read in light of the Old Testament; the Old Testament in light of Jesus Christ. However, the new interpretation does not negate the original meaning. (II.A.6)

> ⟩ In the term "Old Testament," 'old' does not mean that the Jewish Scriptures are outmoded or superseded. For a Christian to read the Old Testament in a spiritual fashion does not cancel the original meaning. The Jewish people are correct to continue reading it according to their own tradition. (II.A.7.22)

> ⟩ There is both continuity and discontinuity in the two testaments – for instance, Christians do not observe purity or dietary laws. But both testaments demand justice and compassion towards the poor,

marginalized, and vulnerable, and insist on fidelity to God alone. The two testaments cannot be played off against one another (C.64.1, 2)

> ➤ A "dynamism of love" animates both testaments. (B.86)

Cosmic Warfare

A yawning chasm of 2,000 years of history and culture separate us from the first-century authors of the Gospels. Their worldview was not at all like ours, nor were many of their social values and practices. We would be appalled at aspects of their culture, as they would be of ours. To understand how they saw the world and the events around them, we must set aside our modern suppositions and attempt to walk for a while in their sandals.

A key aspect of their theological worldview is what scholars call "apocalyptic," from the Greek word *apocalypsis*, which means "revelation." Much of Jewish theology from the second century BCE to the first century CE was apocalyptic in nature; this type of theology flowed directly into the pages of the New Testament. Until we understand that the New Testament is permeated with apocalyptic theology, we will not comprehend its message properly.

Apocalyptic arose during the Maccabean Revolt in 175–167 BCE, when the Jews fought back against Antiochus Epiphanes, the Greek king of Syria. He attempted to destroy Jewish religious and cultural traditions. He forbade circumcision, observance of the Law and the feasts, and his agents tried to force Jews to eat food that was ritually defiling. He also defiled the temple by rededicating it to Zeus Olympias, the Greek god, and slaughtering a pig on the altar. This was referred to in Daniel 9:27; 11:31; and 12:11 as the "desolating sacrilege," and it is picked up again in the New Testament in descriptions of the temple's destruction (Matthew 24:15; Mark 13:14).

Those who were faithful were suffering and dying, while the wicked and those who collaborated with the Greek enemy were prospering. This was not how things were supposed to work! During this period the Book of Daniel was written (although the story is set in the Persian court centuries earlier). It forms the basis of all future apocalyptic, and was intended to give hope and courage to those undergoing persecution. It is a peek behind the veil to the invisible world of the spirit and God's hidden plan. Believers are reassured that God is in control and has not forgotten them. God's intervention into human history is imminent, so patience and perseverance are called for. God is just and faithful, and the fidelity of the believer is not in vain. It was in Daniel that the notion of the bodily resurrection makes its first appearance in the Old Testament. The dead will be raised so that the righteous can be rewarded and the wicked punished:

> At that time Michael, the great prince, the protector of your people, shall arise. There shall be a time of anguish, such as has never occurred since nations first came into existence. But at that time your people shall be delivered, everyone who is found written in the book. Many of those who sleep in the dust of the earth shall awake, some to everlasting life, and some to shame and everlasting contempt. Those who are wise shall shine like the brightness of the sky, and those who lead many to righteousness, like the stars forever and ever. (Daniel 12:1-3)

This passage, which lies at the heart of 1 Thessalonians 4:13-18 and portions of the Book of Revelation, is supposed to occur at the second coming of Christ, which will signal the end of history. In fact, apocalyptic elements are found in Mark 13 (and its parallels in Matthew 24; Luke 21); 1 Corinthians 3:10-15; 15:20-58; 2 Corinthians 5:10; 1 Thessalonians 4:13-18; 2 Thessalonians 1:5-10; Galatians 6:7-9; Romans 2; 1 Peter 4; and 2 Peter 3:10-13. The Book of Revelation is a complete apocalypse from start to finish and is the last book of the New Testament.

There are specific characteristics of apocalyptic theology. There is an emphasis on two ages: the old age that is passing away, and the new one struggling to be born. A good example of this is Galatians 6:7-9 and 2 Corinthians 5:10. Apocalyptic is a black-and-white world: there is good and evil, light and darkness, truth and falsehood – and next to nothing in between! Tribulations and upheavals accompany the turning of the two ages and the approaching end: birthing pains are often used as a metaphor. As the end gets closer, things actually get worse – and this is a sign of hope! With the coming of the end, societies are turned upside down. Think of Mary's praise because God has exalted the lowly and cast down the mighty from their thrones (Luke 1:52-53), as well as the Gospel's insistence that the last shall be first and the first shall be last (Matthew 20:16).

Symbolic language is used: Daniel is filled with bizarre beasts with many eyes and talking horns, and Revelation has its own share of nightmarish beasts and monsters. The text itself explains that these are personifications of earthly powers and empires, such as the Persians, Greeks, and Romans (Daniel 8:20-22). These empires were thought to be the enemies of

God because they had usurped divine power and had taken on claims to divinity. Often someone – usually the author of the book – is whisked away to the heavens for a guided tour. An interpreting angel explains all that is about to happen and what earthly events mean. Think of Paul's heavenly journey in 2 Corinthians 12:1-12: he was taken to the third heaven and heard things that he dared not repeat. Finally, everything must follow a divine script and timetable. Nothing will occur before its allotted time, and all must be in the proper order. At the beginning of Mark's Gospel, Jesus proclaims, "The time [*kairos*, or divine time] is fulfilled!" All the waiting is over; the day of decision has arrived.

Why does all this matter? When we read a 2,000-year-old text that is heavily laden with apocalyptic as if it were a contemporary document describing today's world, we get into trouble. The most obvious examples of this are the fundamentalist sects that anxiously await the return of Jesus and the end times. The *Left Behind* series, based on the Book of Revelation, was a huge success around the time of the turn of the millennium in 2000. The terrifying story was enough to give anyone nightmares, and the Jesus it describes is not the gentle rabbi from Galilee, but a cosmic warrior. Those committed to this view of history are often not overly concerned with improving the social order or preserving the environment. Why bother, if it is all going to end soon?

> Why does all this matter? When we read a 2,000-year-old text that is heavily laden with apocalyptic as if it were a contemporary document describing today's world, we get into trouble.

But there are other, subtler problems. In 1 Corinthians 7, Paul cautions his community to remain in the state in which they were called to faith. If they were married, they should stay that way; if they were single, they should not seek a spouse. If they were slaves when they were called, they should remain so; likewise, if they were free, they should not enslave themselves. A literal and uncontextualized reading of this text caused many to accuse Paul of being anti-marriage and pro-slavery, but nothing could be further from the truth. Paul gives us the reason for his statements: the time is short (7:29), and the form of the present world is passing away (7:31). It was important to be in constant readiness for the end. Most Christians no longer share this expectation of the imminent end, even if they believe it might happen someday. Not many people lie awake at night wondering if this is the world's last night. So how can we base our ethics on a worldview that no longer works for us? We deplore slavery as a great evil and work to eradicate all forms of it. We praise and exalt marriage. And yet the text remains, and many would insist that this is how modern people are to live. The text must be reinterpreted for our own time and situation, rather than slavishly followed or flippantly dismissed.

The Parousia – The Return or Second Coming of Christ

The prime issue in the first century was the return of Christ, or as it is called in the text, the *parousia*. This would herald the end of history and the final judgment (see Mark 13; 15; 1 Thessalonians 4:13-18; 1 Corinthians 15:12-28). The apostles and the first generation of believers were convinced that Jesus would return in their lifetimes. In one verse, Jesus tells his audience, "Truly I tell you, there are some standing here who will not taste death until they see that the kingdom of God has come with power" (Mark 9:1). The Gospels are filled with admonitions to stay awake, sober, and alert, for no one knew the day or the hour of his return. Paul speaks of the "Day of the Lord" in 1 Corinthians: on that day, believers will have to be blameless before him. For this reason, Paul's letters are filled with anxious and sometimes strident moral exhortations.

But Jesus did not return, nor has he done so to this day. The delay of his return touched off a bit of a crisis – we can see this in 2 Peter 3:1-10, where the author urges his readers to pay no heed to the scoffers who ridicule the idea of the Lord's return. He warns them of the suddenness of the end and the catastrophic destruction by fire. As for the question of when this will occur, he explains that with the Lord, one day is like a thousand years. It is no longer helpful to speculate about when these things will occur – the only important thing is to always be in a state of purity and readiness. As years turned into decades, the expectation of the Lord's return receded into the background – always there, but not occupying much of people's consciousness.

The Book of Revelation: Nightmare or Hope?

The Book of Revelation is a troublesome book. At first, it was not universally accepted in the Church. Some thought it was confusing, subject to misinterpretation, and contained none of the teachings of Christ. It has provided fuel for apocalyptic sects and movements for 2,000 years and has been the cause of much grief and violence. Revelation was the basis for David Koresh's Branch Davidian sect in Waco, Texas. He and his followers believed that he was the one worthy to break open the seal of the book in Revelation 5:2-5. In a standoff with ATF agents on April 19, 1993, he and 79 of his followers were killed. This was just the latest in a long string of disturbing movements and events. Many radical ascetical apocalyptic movements existed during the Middle Ages. The language and symbolism of Revelation were a driving force for Martin Luther in the Reformation, and the Peasants' Rebellion that it inspired at that time ended in slaughter and tragedy. In a weird twist, some of the symbolism, such as the "millennium" – a period of a thousand years – was adopted by the Third Reich in Nazi Germany.

> Then I saw in the right hand of the one seated on the throne a scroll written on the inside and on the back, sealed with seven seals; and I saw a mighty angel proclaiming with a loud voice, "Who is worthy to open the scroll and break its seals?" And no one in heaven or on earth or under the earth was able to open the scroll or to look into it. And I began to weep bitterly because no one was found worthy to open the scroll or to look into it. Then one of the elders said to me, "Do not weep. See, the Lion of the tribe of Judah, the Root of David, has conquered, so that he can open the scroll and its seven seals." (Revelation 5:1-5)

How can one book cause so much trouble? The problem is that people have usually read it as predictions of the end of the world and applied it to their own time. Prophecy in the context of Christian worship during the New Testament period was not about predicting the future but offering words of encouragement and admonition in the present. Revelation was written around 96 CE, during the reign of the mad emperor Domitian, who according to some contemporary sources demanded that he be addressed as *dominus et deus* (lord and god).

Revelation encourages and enables the reader (or, more likely in an ancient context, the hearer) to have a transcendent view of the world. By opening the minds and hearts of its audience, the book demonstrates that the world consists of more than meets the eye. It puts the brute force and oppression of the Roman Empire in its proper perspective and exposes the empire for what it really is – a corrupt assuming of divinity. It asks a fundamental question: Who is the Lord of the world? The answer of course, is God: that is demonstrated vividly and dramatically throughout the narrative.

Most scholars believe Revelation was written to encourage those experiencing persecution at the hands of the Roman state. Many of the symbols are expressions of the emperor and the political, economic, and religious power of Rome. They are certainly demonized in the narrative, and in the end are destroyed. Some scholars take an opposing view. The problem is not that the Christians were experiencing persecution – just the opposite. They were lax and quite comfortable within the empire. The goal of the author of Revelation was to fire them up to do battle against Rome.[7] The scholarly consensus, however, is that it was intended to provide hope and courage to beleaguered communities in the face of both persecution and economic and political oppression. One author referred to Rome/Babylon as "a powerful incarnation of international exploitation, oppression, and murder"; this author uses the sacred imagination to create an alternate world and invites the reader/listener to enter it and participate.[8]

Revelation is not a narration of events in our own time. Some present-day TV evangelists read the newspaper in one hand and the Book of Revelation in the other, preaching that everything that happens today was predicted in Revelation and is just a prelude to the horrors and tribulations to come. But that book should certainly not be read in a literal way. It was written for a particular time and place – the eastern Roman Empire in the first century CE – and the circular letter to the seven churches referred to specific conditions and situations. Any interpretation of the text must have been intelligible to the generation of believers to whom it was addressed.

The Roman state used architecture, iconography, art, music, and poetry as instruments of Roman rule and its associated propaganda. Revelation uses similar tools in its effort to deflate the image of the Roman state. The book is filled with visual and symbolic imagery, some of it taken from pagan mythology and some from the Old Testament. For example, images of monsters or dragons are found in all Ancient Near East cultures as well as in the Old Testament.[9]

Some read the text in a way that is not historical, through a poetic, spiritual, or allegorical lens. Others view the book as a long-range script of events facing the Church until the end of time, as if the events of each age have been predicted in the book. During the Reformation, both Catholics and Protestants used Revelation in this way, painting their opponents in its negative imagery. Most people are probably very familiar with what scholars call the "radically futurist" interpretation. This is the stuff of pop eschatology and fundamentalist end-time preachers. Hal Lindsey's famous end-time book *The Late Great Planet Earth* and Tim LaHaye and Jerry Jenkins' *Left Behind* series are the best examples of this category. The time in which the interpreter lives is seen as the last in history: for these authors, the "predictions" in Revelation pertain only to the last few years of world history, and we live in the time just before the final events.[10]

Most modern scholars interpret Revelation as being written in response to unique first-century conditions, and read it in its original historical context. In other words, the events described in the book have already taken place. Again, interpretations cannot be accepted if they would not have been understood by the original readers of the book.

Revelation has been criticized both in the early Church and in our own time. It was not universally accepted at first – some bishops insisted that the book was confusing, difficult to understand, devoid of Christian teachings, and the source of turmoil. More modern critics have pointed first to its savage violence and the image of Christ as the divine warrior. They feel that this text encourages violence and intolerance, and in an age marked by large-scale religious violence, this is a serious consideration. Others point to elements of misogynism in the text – there is the Old Testament image of Jezebel as well as the personification of Babylon (Rome) as the Scarlet Whore or Harlot in chapters 17 and 18. The nightmarish scene that begins at Revelation 19:11 has added fuel to overheated apocalyptic imaginations throughout history and in our own times – just look at the internet and the TV evangelists. This epitomizes cosmic violence and vengeance and links it with Christ the divine warrior:

Then I saw heaven opened, and there was a white horse! Its rider is called Faithful and True, and in righteousness he judges and makes war. His eyes are like a flame of fire, and on his head are many diadems; and he has a name inscribed that no one knows but himself. He is clothed in a robe dipped in blood, and his name is called The Word of God. And the armies of heaven, wearing fine linen, white and pure, were following him on white horses. From his mouth comes a sharp sword with which to strike down the nations, and he will rule them with a rod of iron; he will tread the winepress of the fury of the wrath of God the Almighty. On his robe and on his thigh he has a name inscribed, "King of kings and Lord of lords." Then I saw an angel standing in the sun, and with a loud voice he called to all the birds that fly in midheaven, "Come, gather for the great supper of God, to eat the flesh of kings, the flesh of captains, the flesh of the mighty, the flesh of horses and their riders – flesh of all, both free and slave, both small and great." Then I saw the beast and the kings of the earth with their armies gathered to make war against the rider on the horse and against his army. And the beast was captured, and with it the false prophet who had performed in its presence the signs by which he deceived those who had received the mark of the beast and those who worshipped its image. These two were thrown alive into the lake of fire that burns with sulfur. And the rest were killed by the sword of the rider on the horse, the sword that came from his mouth; and all the birds were gorged with their flesh. (Revelation 19:11-21)

It is very difficult to draw a Christian message from this passage. The Christ figure that it portrays is not likely

3. The New Testament: Many Streams, Many Voices

someone with whom we would want to spend eternity. There is no instruction on love, kindness, mercy, forgiveness, or the Christian life. It is not surprising that many in the early Church were reluctant to admit it to the canon of Scripture.

When we read apocalyptic passages of the Bible in a literal way, we can be overly influenced by its black-and-white, us-against-them attitudes. This can encourage sectarianism, intolerance, and feelings of aggression and hatred, especially towards those whom we fear or who do not belong to our group. It can also generate much uncertainty and fear and make us tend to turn in on ourselves.

> **When we read apocalyptic passages of the Bible in a literal way, we can be overly influenced by its black-and-white, us-against-them attitudes.**

If we know how to read the text, we can benefit from its many gifts. First, it deflates or demythologizes the world's power structures and economic systems. They are not invincible, and we are not their perpetual victims. Nazi Germany and the Soviet Union met their end in due course. Societies, systems, structures, and institutions, including our own, all stand under God's judgment. The message of the text urges us to take a stand and make a commitment. Whom do we serve? The message of apocalyptic is one of hope and patience, especially in the face of persecution and oppression. Both hope and patience are rare commodities in today's world. The most encouraging aspect of apocalyptic is its emphasis on a new creation. Whatever destruction we see in the texts is temporary, and it is always followed by new life and new creation. The world is being renewed, but to accomplish this, aspects of the old world must die.

The New Testament and Doctrine

One of the most unhelpful practices in reading the New Testament is to use it as a quarry for building doctrines, dogmas, and creeds. Unfortunately, this has been a practice for the past 2,000 years, and it shows little sign of abating. Prooftexting is the form this often takes – selectively choosing passages at will to build a case for a particular theological expression. Often the passages chosen are from books written centuries apart, and little if any heed is paid to the passage's historical and cultural context. Five hundred years is a long time and distance when we consider human culture and understanding. Imagine if we were to draw on texts written 500 years earlier than our own time. This would take us back to Elizabethan England – a world quite different from our own. The language would be comprehensible, but with effort; science was in its infancy; explorers had only recently visited the New World; and people were being put on trial and executed for witchcraft or heresy. We cannot just string together a series of verses with similar words or concepts and expect to have a deep and coherent understanding of the modern issue or situation at hand.

Some examples will illustrate what is at stake. In the fourth and fifth centuries CE, a series of Church councils hammered out the doctrines that defined the divinity of Jesus Christ, his relationship to the Father, and the way his two natures – divine and human – were united in one person. Many of the prooftexts for Christ's divinity came from the Gospel of John. At the Council of Nicaea in 325, those who championed the divinity of Christ and his consubstantiality with the Father eagerly pointed to John 10:30, where Jesus stated, "The Father and I are one." It seemed to be an open-and-shut case, but elsewhere in the same Gospel, Jesus said, "the Father is greater than I" (14:28).

The First Council of Nicea, held in 325 in present-day Turkey, was the Church's first ecumenical council. Called by Emperor Constantine, the council discussed several issues, such as the Arianism heresy, and issued decrees on Church matters.

Often orthodox and heterodox theologians would be appealing to the same texts, but with differing interpretations. The point here is that in relying only on Scripture, there is supporting evidence for more than one doctrinal definition. Those who lost the debates – the "heretics" – were not operating out of malice or ill will. They merely saw things differently and were able to find texts to support their position.

The Eucharist presents another example, and correct interpretations of the words of institution are always guaranteed to get arguments started. What did Jesus say at the Last Supper? The institution of the Eucharist is only reported in the three Synoptic Gospels (Matthew, Mark, and Luke) – it is not present in the Gospel of John. Mark is the earliest of the Gospels, written during the period 66–72 CE. Mark 14:22-24 states, "While they were eating, he took a loaf of bread, and after blessing it he broke it, gave it to them, and said, 'Take; this is my body.' Then he took a cup, and after giving thanks he gave it to them, and all of them drank from it. He said to them, 'This is my blood of the covenant, which is poured out for many.'" Note that his blood is poured out for "many" – something that found its way back into the 2010 translation of the Roman Missal, which contains the prayers used at Mass.

As usual, Matthew followed Mark closely, stating in 26:26-28, "While they were eating, Jesus took a loaf of bread, and after blessing it he broke it, gave it to the disciples, and said, 'Take, eat; this is my body.' Then he took a cup, and after giving thanks he gave it to them, saying, 'Drink from it, all of you; for this is my blood of the covenant, which is poured out for many for the forgiveness of sins.'" Notice that the wording is almost the same as in Mark, but Matthew adds "for the forgiveness of sins" to the pouring out of the blood of the covenant.

Luke departs a bit from Mark and Matthew, stating in 22:19-20: "Then he took a loaf of bread, and when he had given thanks, he broke it and gave it to them, saying, 'This is my body, which is given for you. Do this in remembrance of me.' And he did the same with the cup after supper, saying, 'This cup that is poured out for you is the new covenant in my blood.'" Luke expands the statement about the body of Jesus to include "which is given for you." His blood is poured out "for you," instead of for the "many," and it represents the new covenant in his blood. Jesus also told them to do this "in remembrance of me." Also, Luke's institution account has two cups being blessed, which was often the custom in Passover meals.

We can see that there is variation in the three Gospels, but it gets even more complicated. The letters of Paul were written a generation *before* any of the Gospels. In the First Letter to the Corinthians, we find the first New Testament reference to the Eucharist, although Paul calls it "the Lord's Supper." In his argument with members of the community, Paul says,

> For I received from the Lord what I also handed on to you, that the Lord Jesus on the night when he was betrayed took a loaf of bread, and when he had given

thanks, he broke it and said, "This is my body that is for you. Do this in remembrance of me." In the same way he took the cup also, after supper, saying, "This cup is the new covenant in my blood. Do this, as often as you drink it, in remembrance of me." (1 Corinthians 11:23-25)

Paul reports that Jesus said, "this is my body that is for you," with little connotation of sacrifice. Other than that, Paul's account is remarkably close to Luke's narrative. This comparison of texts should caution us not to use the New Testament narratives too rigidly and dogmatically in constructing Eucharistic theology and ritual. There are many ways of expressing the same prayer, and it is more fruitful and helpful to search for the spirit and intent present in the Eucharist rather than minutely examining words for hidden meanings that were never present in the first place.

Hunting through the New Testament for proof of the sacraments is not a helpful undertaking. No one would want to deny the seven sacraments of the Church, but there is not a simple one-to-one correspondence between passages in the New Testament and the seven sacraments. The number of sacraments and the form they have taken have varied over the centuries, and were only firmly established in the time of the Reformation.[11] The two that are beyond question are baptism and the Eucharist. We would be hard pressed to find passages in which Christ explicitly establishes the sacrament of confirmation or holy orders. This does not negate any of the sacraments – their authority flows from the Spirit of Christ present in the Church as it journeys through the challenges of historical experience. A "smoking gun" Scripture passage is not necessary.

For example, the sacrament of penance did not fully develop until the mid-third century, when many who lapsed and denied the faith during persecution wanted to return to full communion. Up until then, baptism removed sin, and it was a one-time affair. Some of the Church Fathers delayed baptism until middle age, hoping that this would give them a better chance at staying on the straight and narrow. After the persecution of the second century, many refused to accept the lapsed back into the fold; there was no second chance. St. Cyprian of Carthage was instrumental in providing opportunities for penance and reconciliation. Even then, it was a long, drawn-out affair, taking months or even a year or more.[12]

In the New Testament, there are provisions for correcting a wayward member and even for expelling them from the community, but nothing that would resemble confession as we know it. There are two places where confession of sins is mentioned: James 5:16 and 1 John 1:9. As we will see, they differ from what we would expect:

> Therefore confess your sins to one another, and pray for one another, so that you may be healed. The prayer of the righteous is powerful and effective. (James 5:16)

> If we confess our sins, he who is faithful and just will forgive us our sins and cleanse us from all unrighteousness. (1 John 1:9)

In the first instance, believers confess to and pray for one another. Confession is communal and open – there is no reference to specific individuals designated for that purpose. In the passage from 1 John, the author does not designate how sins are confessed, or to whom. The focus is on Jesus as the one who cleanses us if we are honest about our need for forgiveness.

The New Testament and Moral Practice

But what about mere moral instruction? The letters of Paul usually close with something called *paraenesis*, or moral exhortation, where the audience was exhorted to do good and avoid evil. To aid them in this endeavour, comprehensive lists were provided of both virtues and vices. The lists were rather standardized and could easily be inserted in any moral treatise. They were not exclusively Jewish or Christian – many similar lists can be found in Greco-Roman moral treatises. This is but one example:

> Do you not know that wrongdoers will not inherit the kingdom of God? Do not be deceived! Fornicators, idolaters, adulterers, male prostitutes, sodomites, thieves, the greedy, drunkards, revilers, robbers – none of these will inherit the kingdom of God. And this is what some of you used to be. But you were washed, you were sanctified, you were justified in the name of the Lord Jesus Christ and in the Spirit of our God. (1 Corinthians 6:9-11)

At the close of the Letter to the Galatians, Paul contrasts two ways of living: one by the spirit and the other by the flesh. This was consistent with the Jewish "two ways" theology found in Deuteronomy and other works. There is a way that leads to life and another that leads to death. Here Paul elaborates these two paths:

> Live by the Spirit, I say, and do not gratify the desires of the flesh. For what the flesh desires is opposed to the Spirit, and what the Spirit desires is opposed to the flesh; for these are opposed to each other, to prevent you from doing what you want. But if you are led by the Spirit, you are not subject to the law. Now the works of the flesh are obvious: fornication, impurity, licentiousness, idolatry, sorcery, enmities, strife, jealousy, anger, quarrels, dissensions, factions, envy, drunkenness, carousing, and things like these. I am warning you, as I warned you before: those who do such things will not inherit the kingdom of God.
>
> By contrast, the fruit of the Spirit is love, joy, peace, patience, kindness, generosity, faithfulness, gentleness, and self-control. (Galatians 5:16-23)

Rather than providing a dogmatic policy statement on each of the listed sins or virtues, Paul's words paint a picture or impression of two opposing ways of life, allowing the reader to choose which path they want to follow. One is oriented towards self-aggrandizement and self-indulgence, while the other is focused on God and service to others. The first is called "living according to the flesh," while the second is "living in the Spirit." The lists are not present to be mined for prooftexts to support opposing opinions on ethical issues.

The early followers of Jesus were certainly not morally lax. It is true that their lists of virtues and vices did not differ a great deal from Greco-Roman moral treatises. One of the key differences was the Christian insistence on the avoidance of these vices and the cultivation of the corresponding virtues. Their moral standards were not suggestions – those who refused to align themselves with this code were not welcome in the community. There is a notorious example in 1 Corinthians 5: a man was discovered living with his father's wife – his stepmother – in a sexual relationship. Not only that, the rest of the community seemed at peace with the situation. This was probably due to a misunderstanding of "Christian freedom," and Paul was quick to set them straight. He was horrified – not even the pagans would tolerate such a thing! It was illegal and punishable under Roman law. In fact, Jewish writers and scholars routinely cast aspersions on the Gentiles precisely because of their alleged sexual immorality. Freedom from the Law does not imply that purity is not a concern: both Paul's communities and those of the Gospels adopted a biblical attitude towards holiness and purity, even if the dietary and purity regulations were not enforced universally. Much of it was based on temple imagery – separating the holy from the unholy.

Paul commanded that the community be called together and his letter be read to everyone. The offender was then to be "delivered up to Satan for destruction of the flesh," a rather dramatic and even sinister way of describing excommunication or expulsion from the community. Drawing on Leviticus 18:8 and Deuteronomy 17:7, Paul was adamant about "driving out the wicked person from among you." He went on to forbid associating with or even eating with immoral people.

In the next chapter of that letter, as we saw above, Paul chastises and warns some community members about other breaches of morality (1 Corinthians 6:9-11).

Many people today ask about mercy and compassion. After all, didn't Jesus eat with tax collectors, prostitutes, and sinners? Paul would counter that Jesus did so to call people to repentance. Once a person has gone through the washing (baptism) and sanctification (spirit), he or she enters a different realm and has a different status. Paul even points out that some of them used to be on that list! What a person used to be no longer matters: after the cleansing of baptism, being found blameless on the Day of the Lord was crucial. Baptism and reception of the Spirit made a person something different – in 2 Corinthians 5:17, Paul says that "if anyone is in Christ, there is a new creation." This term "in Christ" is used extensively in the Pauline letters. It is how the human person participates in the new creation of the cosmos that is taking place. Christ shares his own holiness and perfection with those who remain in him. The holiness of community members was not their own, and sanctity was not a self-help program.

On the surface, it seems to be a clear-cut recipe for moral rigorism. But can this approach be cut and pasted into the 21st-century Church? Only with the greatest difficulty, and for a number of reasons. First, Christianity in the mid-first century CE was a small sect. The community in Corinth at the time the letter was written probably did not number more than 50, and their numbers were perhaps even fewer. The same probably applied to the other communities Paul wrote to in that period. They were small, committed, and tight-knit, and the trust level among them was high. They endured a lot of outside pressure and persecution. All of them were baptized as adults – they had made a conscious, life-altering choice, and were prepared to suffer for it. This is far different from contemporary Christianity as a world religion, where most members inherited their faith, rather than choosing it. The members of any church run the gamut from the zealous and committed to the lethargic or non-participating, with many somewhere in between. Except for a couple of hot-button issues, there is little awareness of having a lifestyle much different from society at large. Much work would have to be done to create a group identity and consciousness.

Early Christian writers were also affected by the culture in which they lived. The letters to the Colossians and the Ephesians, both attributed to Paul but likely not written by him, provide a rather notorious example. At the end of each letter, there is the usual moral exhortation, but with a twist: wives are exhorted to submit to their husbands (something I will discuss below); children to their parents; and slaves to their masters. Granted, the husband is to treat his wife and children with patience and kindness, but there is only one boss. More problematic is the insistence that slaves submit to their masters. As pointed out above, this was a great comfort to slaveowners throughout the centuries. No normal person today would suggest that we return to slavery, for it is rightly regarded as a great evil. But far too many people think this patriarchal and hierarchical order should be the model for family life today. Conservative Christian traditions routinely appeal to these texts to maintain what they perceive to be a biblically modelled family. Ironically, there is little difference between these passages and Greco-Roman treatises of that era on the correct running of a household. The master was lord of his household, holding absolute power – even, in some cases, the power of life and death – over his children, his slaves, and his wife. These pagan written works even urge the master to be benevolent and not too harsh. Colossians and Ephesians borrow attitudes from their surrounding culture and season them with a bit of Christian rhetoric, but the aim is the same: maintain the status quo and run a tight ship. This should be understood as a culturally conditioned bit of advice rather than a divinely ordained model for the household. Just as we do not condone slavery, we look for more equality and mutuality in a marriage than people did in the ancient world.

Reading Paul

Reading the apostle Paul is a challenge. He has quite a reputation – most people love him or hate him. Ironically, their like or dislike is usually for the wrong reasons. Some think he twisted the simple teachings of Jesus – they call him the founder of Christianity, but not in a complimentary or positive sense. Protestants usually view him as a liberator from the oppression of tradition, while Catholics hail him as the founder of Church structures and proper order. To many Jewish people – and even to some Jewish Christians in the early Church – Paul is a renegade from Judaism. Finally, in our own time, many women detest Paul for what they perceive to be his misogynism and oppression of women. Actually, Paul is not any of these things, but it is easy to misunderstand and to misread his letters. Modern Pauline scholarship, sometimes called the "new perspective," strives to let Paul be Paul and understands him as a Second Temple Jew. He should not be read through the lenses of St. Augustine, Martin Luther, or other theological and cultural concerns.

In later centuries, Paul was read through the theological concerns of St. Augustine (354–430) and Martin Luther (1483–1546), both of whom amplified the fallen nature of humanity and the inability of humans to live up to their calling. Luther focused on Paul's insistence that salvation is through faith.

There are several ways *not* to read Paul. First, he does not have the last word on everything – he was right about many things, but spectacularly wrong about others. But we also have to know something about letter writing in the ancient world. Letters were often used to mediate disputes, give orders, and distribute praise and blame. Formal letters, or epistles, as they are called, were designed to make the reader think or act in a particular way. Each letter was written with a rhetorical purpose: it sought to deal with a situation or problem. Paul's letters were not necessarily universal – each letter dealt with a specific problem in a specific community. They were not intended to be Scripture; Paul had no awareness that he was writing part of the New Testament. In fact, his letters were all written before any of the Gospels. The letters he wrote were pastoral and administrative, and were not intended to be theological treatises. The pastoral situation that called for 1 Corinthians to be written was the disunity of the community – their inability to see themselves as forming the body of Christ. His entire letter, even when dealing with diverse issues such as worship, spiritual gifts, sexual ethics, and purity laws, is focused on the disunity of the community and its lack of awareness of their interdependence.

The majority of scholars (not all, to be sure) consider only seven letters to have been written by Paul himself. These are the letters that should be used when reconstructing an outline of Pauline thought: 1 and 2 Corinthians; Romans; Galatians; 1 Thessalonians; Philippians; and Philemon.

But what about the other letters attributed to Paul? These dubious letters, sometimes called deutero-Pauline or pseudo-Pauline, were probably written in the next generation by followers of Paul. His name was attached to these letters to give them additional authority and weight. These letters include 2 Thessalonians, Ephesians, Colossians, and 1 and 2 Timothy. Why are they considered dubious? How are they different from the authentic letters? There are distinct differences in style and vocabulary. Many of these differences are not apparent in English translations, which tend to smooth and harmonize the text, but they are obvious in the Greek originals. These letters also express differences in ecclesiology (church structure) and eschatology (end times). In the authentic letters, Paul is in constant expectation of the imminent "day of the Lord" – Christ's return, the general resurrection and judgment. It is always on the immediate horizon. In letters such as Colossians and Ephesians, it appears that the cosmic event has already taken place. Christ has reconciled the world to himself and reigns supreme as the head of the body – the Church.

The community in 1 Corinthians was a rather free-wheeling place, very spontaneous and charismatic. Women took part in public prophecy and prayer. Paul also commended the many women he regarded as co-workers in his ministry. 1 and 2 Timothy, on the other hand, relegate women to a subordinate status and command them to silence. The community in these two letters was hierarchical and patriarchal; it contained little of the spontaneity and spiritual vibrancy of the authentic letters.

Paul's letters cannot be read as if they are always consistent. Paul can and often is quoted against himself. Since each letter was written in response to a pastoral situation, the rhetorical arguments used in each case may differ when compared to the other letters. A prime example is the image Paul paints of Judaism and the law; this has created the impression that Paul was anti-Judaic and dismissive of the traditions of Israel. One can compile an impressive array of quotations that seem to disparage Israel and the law. But an equally impressive list can be made where he praises Israel and the law and insists that it has value.

Most of the negative quotations are taken from Galatians, which is an angry letter he wrote against "Judaizers" in the Galatian community. They were Jewish Christians who insisted that to be a follower of Jesus, one had to first become a Jew – and that entailed circumcision and observing all the dietary and purity laws. Paul was adamant in his denial of the need for such measures for Gentile converts. In ancient letter writing, the theme of the letter was expressed near the opening lines. It governed the argumentation for the entire letter. Galatians clearly states: "yet we know that a person is justified not by the works of the law but through faith in Jesus Christ. And we have come to believe in Christ Jesus, so that we might be justified by faith in Christ, and not by doing the works of the law, because no one will be justified by the works of the law" (2:16).

For Paul, faith was the new way of identifying with the household of God, rather than observance of the Law. In Galatians, he raged against his opponents, accusing them of making the Gospel of Christ invalid by their insistence on living according to the norms of the age that was passing away.

He therefore pulled out all the rhetorical stops in his effort to show the futility of observance of the Law. With the coming of Christ, humanity had entered a new stage of human history. Many of the barriers and boundary markers between peoples were now being erased or altered. Observance of the Law was the boundary marker between the Jews and the Gentiles, and for Jews, the Law was still in force. But for those who proclaimed their faith in Jesus, it was a different story. The new identifying sign and "entrance requirement" was to be faith. It didn't mean that good deeds were not necessary or useful, but that faith in Jesus was now the way in which one identified with the people of God.

Most of the positive references to Israel and the Law are from the Letter to the Romans. Paul's rhetorical intent responds to a different pastoral problem here. Some Jewish Christians in the Roman community were not keen on Gentile converts, especially if they would not be observing Jewish Law. On the other hand, some Gentile Christians had a smug and superior attitude towards Jewish members of the community. In his letter, Paul shows that neither Jew nor Gentile had lived up to God's expectations. As he put it in Romans 3:23-24, all have fallen short of the glory of God. Paul declared both Jew and Gentile spiritually bankrupt and worthy of condemnation, but then extends the offer of God's salvation to all in Jesus Christ. No one has any claim on God; no one has earned or merits salvation. But to counter the idea that God deserted Israel or has been fickle, Paul insists that Israel has much to be proud of. He agonizes over Israel's refusal of Jesus as the promised Messiah:

For I could wish that I myself were accursed and cut off from Christ for the sake of my own people, my kindred according to the flesh. They are Israelites, and to them belong the adoption, the glory, the covenants, the giving of the law, the worship, and the promises; to them belong the patriarchs, and from them, according to the flesh, comes the Messiah, who is over all, God blessed forever. (Romans 9:3-5)

He finally arrives at the conclusion that their refusal is merely temporary and is part of God's plan to bring the Gentiles on board. In the end, he insists, all Israel will be saved (Romans 11:25).

These examples show that passages from Paul's letters should not be read in isolation from the entire letter from which they are taken. They need to be situated with the pastoral situation that is being addressed and the overall argument that unfolds from the stated theme of the letter. Much confusion results from selecting isolated passages from Paul's letters. This often leads to a distortion of Paul's theological views, and these isolated verses can even be understood in ways entirely opposite from their original intent.

Paul and Women

Nowhere is this more evident than in deciphering Paul's attitudes towards women. He has often been accused of being a misogynist and of providing verses that have been used to oppress women and keep them in a subservient role in the Church. Again, it is necessary to examine all Paul's letters and then each controversial passage in its context. We can only use the seven authentic or undisputed letters of Paul in retrieving his teaching on women. In 1 Corinthians 11:4, Paul says, "Any man who prays or prophesies with something on his head disgraces his head, but any woman who prays or prophesies with her head unveiled disgraces her head – it is one and the same thing as having her head shaved." He is assuming that women and men pray and prophesy together – that is not the issue. He is concerned with decorum and appearances – women should be properly attired when prophesying. He also wants to avoid confusion with the various Greco-Roman religious cults that were prevalent in Corinth. They often included ecstatic, frenzied forms of worship. His concern with proper attire is culturally conditioned. Today we might hear a similar homily railing against wearing tank tops or short shorts at liturgy.

Most of Paul's negative reputation in this area stems from one notorious passage, quoted here in full:

> What should be done then, my friends? When you come together, each one has a hymn, a lesson, a revelation, a tongue, or an interpretation. Let all things be done for building up. If anyone speaks in a tongue, let there be only two or at most three, and each in turn; and let one interpret. But if there is no one to interpret, let them be silent in church and speak to themselves and to God. Let two or three prophets speak, and let the others weigh what is said. If a revelation is made to someone else sitting nearby, let the first person be silent. For you can all prophesy one by one, so that all may learn and all be encouraged. And the spirits of prophets are subject to the prophets, for God is a God not of disorder but of peace.

(As in all the churches of the saints, women should be silent in the churches. For they are not permitted to speak, but should be subordinate, as the law also says. If there is anything they desire to know, let them ask their husbands at home. For it is shameful for a woman to speak in church. Or did the word of God originate with you? Or are you the only ones it has reached?)

Anyone who claims to be a prophet, or to have spiritual powers, must acknowledge that what I am writing to you is a command of the Lord. Anyone who does not recognize this is not to be recognized. So, my friends, be eager to prophesy, and do not forbid speaking in tongues; but all things should be done decently and in order. (1 Corinthians 14:26-40)

First of all we need to look at verses 26 to 40 as a whole. The emphasis and concern is public worship that reflects decency and order. In verse 33, Paul insists that God is a God not of disorder but of peace. In verse 39, he reiterates this: "So be eager to prophesy, and do not forbid speaking in tongues, but all things should be done decently and in order." The context for this is the chaos and bedlam of Corinthian communal prayer. It could easily be confused with pagan ecstatic religious expressions. Prayer of this type is characterized by frenzied shouting, screaming, and as Paul describes elsewhere, babbling. Notice that he emphasizes speaking in order, and not more than one person at a time. Earlier, in 1 Corinthians 11:5, it is assumed that a woman will pray and prophesy in the assembly. If we take this apparent prohibition literally and universally, then Paul has just contradicted himself. In fact, he is attempting to bring order and decorum to the assembly, rather than suppressing or stifling anyone. But what about the two notorious verses – the "women be silent" ones? In some of the earliest hand-copied manuscripts of this letter, verses 33b to 35 are tacked on to the end of the chapter. Other manuscripts have curious notations next to these verses, perhaps signalling that something is amiss. A near-identical parallel is found in 1 Timothy 2:11-12, which is a much later pseudo-Pauline work. By then, Church structures had already begun to evolve, and more emphasis was being placed on order. In that letter, women are clearly given a subservient role and their voices are stifled. There is a strong possibility that the words from 1 Timothy 2:11-12 were written in the margins of 1 Corinthians 14 at a much later date (a common practice, called "glossing the text"), eventually being recopied into the text itself. If the words are Paul's, they are addressed to the behaviour of a particular group of women at Corinth, and are intended to keep order in the assembly, rather than being a universal principle.

Strangely, considering the reputation Paul has for misogyny, he was effusive and complimentary about the women with whom he engaged in ministry. At the end of his letters, he often tacks on a list of people to whom he sends greetings. These are seldom read today – they are about as exciting as the genealogies of Jesus in the Gospels – but they contain some interesting information. For instance, in Romans 16:1-16, Paul greets many people, including several prominent women. In 16:1, he commends to them "our sister Phoebe, a deacon of the church at Cenchreae, so that you may welcome her in the Lord as is fitting for the saints, and help her in whatever she may require from you, for she has been a benefactor of many and of myself as well."

Obviously, Paul thinks highly of her and she has been a great help to him. She is also a deacon – yes, there were women deacons in the early Church. This is interesting in light of Pope Francis' recent decision to appoint a commission to study the possible role of female deacons in the Church. Paul also greets "Prisca and Aquila, who work with me in Christ Jesus, and who risked their necks for my life, to whom not only I give thanks, but also all the churches of the Gentiles" (16:3-4). This was a married couple that worked extensively with Paul; they are also mentioned in Acts 18:2-3, 18, 26 and in 1 Corinthians 16:19. He also greets "Mary, who has worked very hard among you" (Romans 16:6) and "those workers in the Lord, Tryphaena and Tryphosa" (Romans 16:12). The bombshell comes in verse 7: "Greet Andronicus and Junia, my relatives who were in prison with me; they are prominent among the apostles, and they were in Christ before I was."

Junia is a woman's name, and yet she is called an apostle. The term "apostle" was used to refer to people beyond the group of 12 whom Jesus called. The Twelve were all apostles, but not all apostles belonged to the Twelve. There was a translation problem due to the nature of the Greek language. Junia is the direct object in this sentence, so the ending of the word changes to "Junian." If this individual were male, it would also be "Junian," but it would have a circumflex accent (ˆ) over the final vowel. The ancient sources attest to the feminine reading well into the early Middle Ages, especially in the East. In the fourth century, the Church Father John Chrysostom, who was hardly a feminist, praised the "wisdom of this woman who was honored with the title apostle."

St. John Chrysostom (347–407), who served as archbishop of Constantinople, is a doctor (teacher) of the Church. He is known for his scriptural homilies and other sermons.

Knowledge of Greek rapidly died out in the West, and there was a near total reliance on the Latin Vulgate translation. The name came to be read as Junias (masculine) rather than Junia (feminine), which led to some amusing translations: the King James version has Junia, but the New International Version and the Revised Standard Version render it Junias – Junia becomes a man! The New Revised Standard Version – used in the Canadian lectionary (book of readings used at Mass) – restores the feminine gender to poor Junia. Although opinions are divided, most scholarship supports this reading. This is another example of how women are often written out of the text.

There are two final passages that are informative. In Colossians 4:15, "Paul" (or whoever wrote the letter) asks that his greetings be given to "the brothers and sisters in Laodicea, and to Nympha and the church in her house." The early Christians met in houses – there were no churches in our sense of the word; this reference sheds light on the role women often had as leaders of house churches. In Philippians 4:2, Paul urges Euodia and Syntyche to "be of the same mind in the Lord." He then asks that his companion "help these women, for they have struggled beside me in the work of the gospel." The takeaway from an examination of these passages is that women were actively involved in ministry and spreading the gospel, and that Paul worked closely with many of them. This would be strange behaviour indeed if Paul were the misogynist that some claim him to be.

The New Testament and Sexuality

What does the New Testament teach about homosexuality? It doesn't have a lot to say. To be sure, none of the writers (mostly Paul) look with favour on it, but they are equally condemning of all forms of sexual immorality. In chapter 1 of Romans, Paul condemns Gentiles for their failure to know and obey God. He claims that the created order provides a sufficient revelation of God, but they worshipped creation rather than the creator. Because of this root sin – idolatry – their minds became clouded and they surrendered to deviant sexual desires. God let them go their way, and the whole range of human sins was the result: "They were filled with every kind of wickedness, evil, covetousness, malice. Full of envy, murder, strife, deceit, craftiness, they are gossips, slanderers, God-haters, insolent, haughty, boastful, inventors of evil, rebellious toward parents, foolish, faithless, heartless, ruthless" (Romans 1:29-31). The major sin was idolatry, which is Paul's target; homosexuality and the long list of other sins were the consequences of the loss of God-consciousness. Paul looks at the broken human condition and then both asks and answers the question: Where does this come from?

In the Old Testament, Leviticus condemns homosexual acts, but as part of a long list of sexual sins such as incest, child sacrifice, and witchcraft. Sexual immorality of all forms causes the land to have "vomited out its inhabitants" (Leviticus 18:25-28).

Here we must examine the long and complicated tradition that begins with the story of the destruction of Sodom and

Gomorrah in Genesis 18 and 19. God told Abraham that reports of the extreme wickedness of these two cities had reached his ears, and God was sending a couple of angelic agents to investigate before destroying them. Abraham pleaded with God on behalf of the cities, asking if God would destroy them if he could find even 50 righteous people in them. God relented – for 50 righteous he would not destroy them. Abraham bargained with him from 50, to 40, 30, 20, and finally 10, and God agreed – for 10 righteous individuals, he would spare the cities. Later, the two angels lodge with Abraham's nephew Lot in Sodom. A huge crowd formed outside the door, demanding that Lot bring out the two strangers so that the mob might "know" them. (This Hebrew word, *yadah*, means "to know," but is often used to connote sexual intercourse.) In this context, intercourse would have been gang rape. In response, Lot offered the mob his two virgin daughters instead, but they had set their sights on the two incognito angels, who finally struck them all blind. The offering of the two daughters is appalling to most people and is further evidence of how much our culture differs from that of the ancients. Apparently, even 10 righteous individuals could not be found, so both cities were utterly destroyed in fire and sulfur.

The fate of Sodom and Gomorrah became a watchword for what God would do to sinful and impenitent people. It is repeated several times in the New Testament (Romans 9:29; 2 Peter 2:4-10; Jude 1:7; Revelation 11:7-8; and Matthew 10:1-5), usually stating that the fate of those two cities would be nothing in comparison to the fate of the cities that rejected Jesus.

So, what was the sin of Sodom? Some Jewish sources, and most of the later Christian authors, identified it with homosexuality. A careful look at the biblical sources, however, paints a much more nuanced picture. Sexual sins are not at the top of Sodom's charge sheet. Ezekiel 16:48-50 has a completely different take:

> As I live, says the Lord GOD, your sister Sodom and her daughters have not done as you and your daughters have done. This was the guilt of your sister Sodom: she and her daughters had pride, excess of food, and prosperous ease, but did not aid the poor and needy. They were haughty, and did abominable things before me; therefore I removed them when I saw it.

There is no explicit mention of anything sexual – rather, greed, pride, and contempt for the poor were their downfall. According to Sirach 16:8, God loathed Sodom on account of their arrogance. In 3 Maccabees 2:5, the author says of God, "You consumed with fire and sulfur the people of Sodom who acted arrogantly, who were notorious for their vices; and you made them an example to those who should come afterward."

Rabbinic sources had a similar view – the Babylonian Talmud, written in the period 200–500 CE, contained horrifying legends about the people in Sodom, especially how they would torture and abuse travellers and strangers. According to one, a daughter of Lot was burned alive for giving bread to a beggar, while another woman was covered with honey and stung to death by bees for giving water to someone passing through. Robbery, extortion, and rape of strangers, male or female, was a common practice for the inhabitants of Sodom. Inhabitants would routinely refuse food, water, and shelter to travellers. Hospitality in the Ancient Near East was sacred and inviolable – this unwelcoming behaviour would have been viewed as an abomination and offense against God.

This suggests that one must use the Bible with great care when discussing ethical issues. Passages cannot be plucked at will to bolster arguments for or against anything, especially with regard to sexuality, marriage, or the structures of families.

Customs and structures have varied throughout time. The patriarchs had many wives, as well as concubines. We can call to mind Hagar the slave girl, whom Sarah gave to Abraham so that he might have an heir. Jacob had two wives – Rachel and Leah – as well as concubines, and he had children by all of them. According to 1 Kings 11:1-4, Solomon loved many foreign women, and had 700 wives and 300 concubines. The only note of reproach in the account was that they enticed Solomon to worship their foreign gods.

Central to the biblical view of sexuality was the preservation and channelling of the life force. Offspring were extremely important, for in an era that did not believe in an afterlife, one lived on through descendants. To be childless was a curse; to die childless was virtual annihilation. The Levirate law in Deuteronomy 25:5-10 decreed that if a man died childless, his brother was expected to father children through his widow. To refuse to do so was a great disgrace.

The Levirate Law generated the trick question that the Sadducees posed to Jesus concerning the resurrection in the case of a woman married consecutively to seven brothers (Mark 12:18-27; Matthew 22:23-33; Luke 20:27-40). Purity of the blood line and the survival of the people was a driving force behind much of the Old Testament sexual legislation.

Related to this is the story of Onan in Genesis 38:1-11: Onan was supposed to father children for his dead brother by having intercourse with his widow, following the Levirate law. This was to ensure that his name would live on through descendants. Realizing that the children would belong to his dead brother and that he would have no inheritance, he withdrew before completing the act and "spilled his seed on the ground." God struck him down in anger, according to the text. It is likely that Onan's sin was his unwillingness to perform his duty for his dead brother – a grievous sin. Later Jewish and Christian traditions interpreted the sin for which he was punished as masturbation, but that interpretation is not really borne out by the text or by knowledge of the laws and customs of the times. And it is nowhere specifically mentioned in the New Testament.

Virginity was a supreme value for a young woman, especially to her father's honour. In Deuteronomy 22:20-21, a woman found not to be a virgin on her wedding day could be stoned to death. The same applied to cases of adultery, the violation of the seventh commandment. These measures were still in force to some degree in the New Testament, which explains Joseph's decision to divorce Mary quietly, so as not to put her in danger of the law's full force. In John 7:53–8:11, the woman taken in adultery was in danger of being stoned, although Leviticus 18:20, 20:10, and Deuteronomy 22:22 decree that both the man and the woman would be put to death. It is illuminating that in both these cases in the New Testament, the response was mercy and compassion.

Violence and Retribution: An Eye for an Eye

The same applies to issues of violence, especially retribution for personal injury or the conduct of warfare. Many who support capital punishment and aggressive, rigorous forms of punishment appeal to passages such as Exodus 21:23-25: "If any harm follows, then you shall give life for life, eye for eye, tooth for tooth, hand for hand, foot for foot, burn for burn, wound for wound, stripe for stripe." This was originally intended to be a principle of limitation and proportion, preventing blood feuds and vendettas. One may take *no more than* an eye, hand, or foot – burning down a village and killing its inhabitants was not acceptable. Unlike the time in which these books were written, we have a legal system, and that is where justice is to be sought today.

Those who burn down cities and kill civilian inhabitants during wartime are later put on trial (we hope) for war crimes – they cannot claim divine sanction for their deeds (although many try). What may have made sense in a nomadic culture millennia ago no longer fits into our worldview and experience. In the Sermon on the Mount, Jesus recast this principle in a startling and radical fashion:

> "You have heard that it was said, 'An eye for an eye and a tooth for a tooth.' But I say to you, Do not resist an evildoer. But if anyone strikes you on the right cheek, turn the other also; and if anyone wants to sue you and take your coat, give your cloak as well; and if anyone forces you to go one mile, go also the second mile. Give to everyone who begs from you, and do not refuse anyone who wants to borrow from you." (Matthew 5:38-42)

Morality and ethics evolve along with experience and the deepening of understanding.

Both the Old and New Testaments have an uncompromising code of proper sexual behaviour. Most of it still stands, even if in theory rather than practice. In drawing on the Scriptures for guidance in matters of sexuality – and in other areas, too – modern understandings of biology, anthropology, and psychology must also be joined to the discussion. Both the Old and New Testaments have a rather one-dimensional view of sin – they tended to concentrate on the act, rather than the person and the intent. We have a broader and deeper understanding of the complex and at times ambiguous nature of the human person. We are more aware of the role of the formative years of a person's life, as well as the influences of culture and society. Not all negative behaviour can be attributed to malice or ill will, just as not all "good" behaviour is a sign of holiness or moral superiority.

> Both the Old and New Testaments have a rather one-dimensional view of sin – they tended to concentrate on the act, rather than the person and the intent. We have a broader and deeper understanding of the complex and at times ambiguous nature of the human person.

The New Testament and Salvation

The Bible – especially the New Testament – is often used to determine who is "saved" and who is not. It can be treated like the shortlist for heaven, and many passages can be interpreted in this way. But once again, things are not so simple. This verse from the Acts of the Apostles is the focal point for controversy: "There is salvation in no one else, for there is no other name under heaven given among mortals by which we must be saved" (Acts 4:12). That sounds clear enough – there is no hope for anyone not calling upon the name of Jesus. In various passages, Paul speaks of "those who are being saved" and "those who are perishing."

This is part of the apocalyptic scheme of salvation – the Day of the Lord. In the Old Testament, it was the time when Israel and the nations would be judged. It was to be a terrifying day, even for those on the right side. In passages such as Joel 2:28, quoted in Acts 2, all those calling on the name of the Lord – YHWH, the God of Israel – would be saved. Peter and the first community of Jesus' followers firmly believed that the final judgment, heralded by the return of Christ, was just around the corner – it would happen within their lifetimes. This judgment and consummation of history would destroy all that was not in harmony with God. Does this make sense outside of an apocalyptic view of history and theology?

> Then afterward I will pour out my spirit on all flesh;
> your sons and your daughters shall prophesy,
> your old men shall dream dreams,
> and your young men shall see visions.
> (Joel 2:28)

John's Gospel is uncompromising – it is only by believing that Jesus is the one sent from above that one can experience eternal life. Those who do not respond with faith bring judgment on themselves:

"For God so loved the world that he gave his only Son, so that everyone who believes in him may not perish but may have eternal life.

Indeed, God did not send the Son into the world to condemn the world, but in order that the world might be saved through him. Those who believe in him are not condemned; but those who do not believe are condemned already, because they have not believed in the name of the only Son of God." (John 3:16-18)

> John 3:16 is probably one of the most well-known passages in the New Testament: "For God so loved the world that he gave his only Son, so that everyone who believes in him may not perish but may have eternal life."

And yet with this same Gospel, Jesus hints that his saving mission touches on more than the immediate community: "Now is the judgment of this world; now the ruler of this world will be driven out. And I, when I am lifted up from the earth, will draw all people to myself" (John 12:31-32). In the letters of John, the strongest language is reserved not for unbelievers, but for those who used to be members of their community but chose another faith path. In fact, this is the only place in the New Testament where the term "antichrist" is used, and it refers to fellow Christians (1 John 2:18-28).

But other voices have a more nuanced view – sometimes those same voices that spoke of doom and destruction. The well-known story of the judgment of the nations from Matthew 25 is but one example:

"When the Son of Man comes in his glory, and all the angels with him, then he will sit on the throne of his glory. All the nations will be gathered before him, and he will separate people one from another as a shepherd separates the sheep from the goats, and he will put the sheep at his right hand and the goats at the left. Then the king will say to those at his right hand, 'Come, you that are blessed by my Father, inherit the kingdom prepared for you from the foundation of the world; for I was hungry and you gave me food, I was thirsty and you gave me something to drink, I was a stranger and you welcomed me, I was naked and you gave me clothing, I was sick and you took care of me, I was in prison and you visited me.' Then the righteous will answer him, 'Lord, when was it that we saw you hungry and gave you food, or thirsty and gave you something to drink? And when was it that we saw you a stranger and welcomed you, or naked and gave you clothing? And when was it that we saw you sick or in prison and visited you?' And the king will answer them, 'Truly I tell you, just as you did it to one of the least of these who are members of my family, you did it to me.' Then he will say to those at his left hand, 'You that are accursed, depart from me into the eternal fire prepared for the devil and his angels; for I was hungry and you gave me no food, I was thirsty and you gave me nothing to drink, I was a stranger and you did not welcome me, naked and you did not give me clothing, sick and in prison and you did not visit me.' Then they also will answer, 'Lord, when was it that we saw you hungry or thirsty or a stranger or naked or sick or in prison, and did not take care of you?' Then he will answer them, 'Truly I tell you, just as you did not do it to one of the least of these, you did not do it to me.' And these will go away into eternal punishment, but the righteous into eternal life." (Matthew 25:31-46)

There are some very interesting aspects to this story. First, those who were ushered into God's kingdom were not conscious of having done anything exceptional, nor were their good deeds at all religious in the conventional sense of the term. They merely took note of basic human needs and responded with active, hands-on compassion. Meanwhile, those excluded from the kingdom were indignant, for they were not aware of any lack in their religious observance or devotion to the Lord. The reply of the Lord was identical in both instances: what you have done or not done to the least of my brothers and sisters, you have done or not done to me. The failure of the excluded group was their absence of practical love or compassion. Remember that this was the judgment of both Israel and the nations – the Gentiles – and the expectation was that the nations would not fare well. But it was also the expectation of the early Christians that their expressed faith in Jesus was sufficient. This story bursts all of those bubbles. All those who respond in a compassionate and just manner to the needs of fellow human beings are welcome in God's kingdom – mere membership in the "right" group or having the "right" faith counts for little.

Despite Paul's division of humanity into those who are being saved and those who are perishing, he extends hope to those who are neither Jew nor Christian. In his searing indictment of humanity, both Jew and Gentile, he arrived at the conclusion that all have fallen short of the glory of God and that no one merits or can claim righteousness or salvation. He admits that those who obey the law of God written in their hearts are not necessarily excluded from God's salvation.

> For it is not the hearers of the law who are righteous in God's sight, but the doers of the law who will be justified. When Gentiles, who do not possess the law, do instinctively what the law requires, these, though not having the law, are a law to themselves. They show that what the law requires is written on their hearts, to which their own conscience also bears witness; and their conflicting thoughts will accuse or perhaps excuse them on the day when, according to my gospel, God, through Jesus Christ, will judge the secret thoughts of all. (Romans 2:13-16)

The question of salvation is a difficult one – the Church has struggled with it for two millennia. At various times in its history, especially in the Middle Ages, the Church has declared that only Catholic Christians in good standing will be saved and that Jews, Muslims, pagans, schismatics, and heretics are destined for the lake of fire reserved for the devil and his angels. This is not what the Church teaches today, but unfortunately, too many still believe it. While still holding that salvation is through Christ, *Lumen Gentium* acknowledged that only those who rejected Christ and the Church with full knowledge that they were necessary for salvation would be denied. The document further recognizes, drawing on writers going back to St. Augustine, that merely being a member of the Church does not guarantee salvation. Likewise, not belonging to it does not automatically condemn a person to hell.

> *Lumen Gentium* (A Light for the Nations) is the document on the Church published in 1964, during the Second Vatican Council. Its aim is to explain the Church's nature and clarify that its mission is to all people.

The point here is that there is no "smoking gun" passage in Scripture, one way or another. People grappled with the question then, just as they do now. Scripture must be joined with reflection, dialogue, experience, and prayer – flipping open a bible for an appropriate passage to end all argument simply will not do. Our collective experience over the past 2,000 years must also be considered, along with the understanding and respect gained in honest and humble dialogue with followers of other religious traditions.

> The point of all this is that there is no "smoking gun" passage in Scripture, one way or another. People grappled with the question then, just as they do now. Scripture must be joined with reflection, dialogue, experience, and prayer – flipping open a bible for an appropriate passage to end all argument simply will not do.

The Chain of Love

If the New Testament does not intend to give us a list of rules, then how does it guide us? Are we simply adrift in a sea of moral and historical relativism? Not at all. There is a thread

– more of a golden chain – that runs through all of the New Testament writings. The chain is love: not a warm and fuzzy feeling, but an unceasing concern for the well-being and happiness of others and for the common good.

Paul, as usual, says it well:

If I speak in the tongues of mortals and of angels, but do not have love, I am a noisy gong or a clanging cymbal. And if I have prophetic powers, and understand all mysteries and all knowledge, and if I have all faith, so as to remove mountains, but do not have love, I am nothing. If I give away all my possessions, and if I hand over my body so that I may boast, but do not have love, I gain nothing.

Love is patient; love is kind; love is not envious or boastful or arrogant or rude. It does not insist on its own way; it is not irritable or resentful; it does not rejoice in wrongdoing but rejoices in the truth. It bears all things, believes all things, hopes all things, endures all things.

Love never ends. But as for prophecies, they will come to an end; as for tongues, they will cease; as for knowledge, it will come to an end. For we know only in part, and we prophesy only in part; but when the complete comes, the partial will come to an end. When I was a child, I spoke like a child, I thought like a child, I reasoned like a child; when I became an adult, I put an end to childish ways. For now we see in a mirror, dimly, but then we will see face to face. Now I know only in part;

then I will know fully, even as I have been fully known. And now faith, hope, and love abide, these three; and the greatest of these is love. (1 Corinthians 13:1-13)

He has just finished giving a tongue-lashing to the Corinthian community for their failure in these areas. Every word he uses to describe love is what they are not. Love is maturity, patience, kindness, humility, and selflessness.

He also says it well in his letter to the Romans:

Let love be genuine; hate what is evil, hold fast to what is good; love one another with mutual affection; outdo one another in showing honour. Do not lag in zeal, be ardent in spirit, serve the Lord. Rejoice in hope, be patient in suffering, persevere in prayer. Contribute to the needs of the saints; extend hospitality to strangers.

Bless those who persecute you; bless and do not curse them. Rejoice with those who rejoice, weep with those who weep. Live in harmony with one another; do not be haughty, but associate with the lowly; do not claim to be wiser than you are. Do not repay anyone evil for evil, but take thought for what is noble in the sight of all. If it is possible, so far as it depends on you, live peaceably with all. Beloved, never avenge yourselves, but leave room for the wrath of God; for it is written, "Vengeance is mine, I will repay, says the Lord." No, "if your enemies are hungry, feed them; if they are thirsty, give them something to drink; for by doing this you will heap burning coals on their heads." Do not be overcome by evil, but overcome evil with good. (Romans 12:9-2)

He follows with a laser-like focus on love's importance:

> Owe no one anything, except to love one another; for the one who loves another has fulfilled the law. The commandments, "You shall not commit adultery; You shall not murder; You shall not steal; You shall not covet"; and any other commandment, are summed up in this word, "Love your neighbour as yourself." Love does no wrong to a neighbour; therefore, love is the fulfilling of the law. (Romans 13:8-10)

At the very core of the New Testament's love ethic is the question presented to Jesus about which of the commandments was the greatest:

> One of the scribes came near and heard them disputing with one another, and seeing that [Jesus] answered them well, he asked him, "Which commandment is the first of all?" Jesus answered, "The first is, 'Hear, O Israel: the Lord our God, the Lord is one; you shall love the Lord your God with all your heart, and with all your soul, and with all your mind, and with all your strength.' The second is this, 'You shall love your neighbour as yourself.' There is no other commandment greater than these." Then the scribe said to him, "You are right, Teacher; you have truly said that 'he is one, and besides him there is no other'; and 'to love him with all the heart, and with all the understanding, and with all the strength,' and 'to love one's neighbour as oneself,' – this is much more important than all whole burnt offerings and sacrifices." When Jesus saw

that he answered wisely, he said to him, "You are not far from the kingdom of God." After that no one dared to ask him any question. (Mark 12:28-34; parallels in Matthew 22:34-40 and Luke 10:25-28)

Of course, this was nothing new. Jesus quoted from Deuteronomy 6:4 and joined it with Leviticus 19:18. Everything needed was already in the tradition, and there are no grounds for playing the two testaments off against one another. They are teaching the same thing. At the end of Luke's version, Jesus tells the parable of the Good Samaritan in answer to the lawyer's query about who was his neighbour. Jesus asked them who was the neighbour to the man left for dead by the roadside. They acknowledged that it was the one who showed him mercy or compassion. Jesus concludes the story with a command that answers our questions about how to live: Go and do likewise!

For Further Reflection

1. The different Gospel accounts of Jesus' passion, death, and resurrection illustrate very well the way history was recorded in ancient times. What are some of the differences in these accounts? Why might these differences exist?

2. The Jewish uprising against Rome in 66–73 AD and the resulting defeat had devastating effects on the Jewish people, especially the destruction of the temple in 70 CE. How is the destruction of the temple reflected in the Gospel narratives? How important is it that we read the

Gospels with an awareness that the evangelists are writing at least 40 years after the crucifixion?

3. Reflect on anti-Semitism throughout history and discuss how misunderstanding the Gospel writers' intentions has resulted in violence and the persecution of the Jewish people. This highlights the importance of sound biblical scholarship.

4. It is important for Christians to read and respect the Old Testament. The document *The Jewish People and Their Sacred Scriptures in the Christian Bible* contains many recommendations for a Christian understanding of the Old Testament and its role in salvation history. Reflect on prophecy in the Old Testament and the way the New Testament writers "read backwards" as they sought to shed light on their own experience with Jesus.

5. What is apocalyptic theology and how has it influenced the writing of the New Testament? How are we to interpret these apocalyptic writings? How have they influenced the thinking of Christians today?

6. The letters of Paul address moral practice for the Christian community, which was very small in the mid-first century. What types of issues were addressed and how did the behaviour expected differ from behaviour that was acceptable in the culture of the time? Would this moral instruction be compatible in our culture today? Why or why not?

7. Which New Testament letters do scholars agree have been written by Paul? What about the others? Why were they attributed to Paul? What was the purpose of writing letters to the early Church? Provide an example of a letter that was written for a specific purpose and explain why it was written.

8. Paul's writings on women have caused much controversy. What are some of the controversial passages and how do we resolve these issues to get to the reason why Paul is sending these particular messages to certain communities? In reality, does it seem that Paul includes women in the work of the gospel?

Conclusion

Encountering Rather than Reading the Bible

An 1,800-year-old papyrus document found in 1941 near Cairo contains the transcript of a dialogue between the Church Father Origen and a group of bishops.[1] In exasperation, Origen blurts out, "I beseech you, therefore, be transformed!" He was referring to the need to rise above our more primitive natures and selfish desires and to become like Christ – that is how he read the Scriptures. Christ is ever present throughout the Scriptures; we seek and find him in order to be transformed. This is when our roots sink deeply into the silent, powerful river that glides below the surface of the Scriptures. Throughout history there has been a tension between those who do just that and those who read the Bible in a superficial manner or use it in ways for which it was never intended.

There are hints of this in the New Testament – especially when Paul tells his readers to put on the mind and heart of Christ (1 Corinthians 2:6; Philippians 2:5ff; Romans 12:2). Being a Christian does not mean business as usual. We are here on earth for one reason: to learn how to love and serve, with everything that entails. If we reach the end of our lives in the same spiritual state that we began it with, then we have failed miserably.

Delving into the Scriptures is more than just reading a book – it is a process in which we take part. We draw nourishment and sustenance from the Scriptures. Praying and meditating with them transforms and forms the sacred imagination. Many people are reluctant to associate the imagination with the spiritual life – after all, it's "just" our imagination; it's not "real." But the sacred imagination can be more real and more meaningful than so-called reality, for it forms our view of the world, God, other people, and our place in the cosmos. It would be helpful to get over our fear of the imagination and our reluctance to allow it into our spiritual journey.

Imaginative engagements with Scripture are meant to transform our consciousness – to create a new interior life. As part of this process, our emotions are also brought into play. What did you feel – in your emotions and in your body – when you meditated on a particular passage? Ignatius of Loyola tells us to create the scene in our imagination and place ourselves within it, not as an observer but as an active participant. Take the role of one of the characters, interacting with this figure and that one and listening for what they may tell you. Do this for all the characters in a story – even the rather unsavoury ones! The movements of the Spirit within you – your inner feelings, sensations, and reactions – will guide and instruct you. Following an ancient tradition of the interior senses, Ignatius urges us to taste and savour not only the words of Scripture but the divinity itself that is found in such scenes as the nativity. Even within Scripture, the senses are called upon to experience rather than intellectualize the text:

He said to me, Mortal, eat this scroll that I give you and fill your stomach with it. Then I ate it; and in my mouth it was as sweet as honey. (Ezekiel 3:3)

How sweet are your words to my taste, sweeter than honey to my mouth! (Psalm 119:103)

Your words were found, and I ate them, and your words became to me a joy and the delight of my heart; for I am called by your name, O LORD, God of hosts. (Jeremiah 15:16)

The practice of *lectio divina* calls for the reading of a passage several times, slowly, savouring and tasting the words, and allowing them to nourish the heart, mind, and soul. Most of all, engagement with Scripture is not reading a book, and it is not an accumulation of facts. It is more a matter of immersing ourselves in the story and allowing it to carry us along by the current. We enter into Scripture so it can enter into us.

The Bible is about us: no one else. Rather than using it as a weapon or measuring stick with which to judge others, we can recognize it for what it is: a mirror of the soul. We meet all sorts of characters in the Bible – heroes, villains, and many in between. And we are all of them! Instead of looking down on the Pharisees, denouncing the tax collectors, or booing and hissing at Herod or Pilate, we may become aware that there is a bit of each one of these characters in each of us. They are a collection of human attitudes and weaknesses, and we are certainly not immune. Have we ever felt threatened and tempted to snuff out the light in others as Herod did? Have we ever failed to do what we knew was right because of fear, like Pontius Pilate? Have we ever misused power for our own ends, like King David?

> The Bible is about us, no one else. Rather than using it as a weapon or measuring stick with which to judge others, we can recognize it for what it is: a mirror of the soul. We meet all sorts of characters in the Bible – heroes, villains, and many in between. And we are all of them!

The good news is that we are also the "good" characters in the Bible. As we meditate on the scenes in which Jesus heals and encourages others, we may recognize that we too respond in these ways, however imperfectly. And the consolation we receive during these reflections and meditations can inspire us to go beyond ourselves and do likewise.

The Bible is a collection of stories. This statement alone can generate uneasiness in people, for we equate stories with things that are not true. Many years ago, a film about Jesus (based on a book) was titled *The Greatest Story Ever Told*. And that is correct – it is a story in the best sense of the word. Whenever Jesus was asked a question, he responded with a story or a parable. That was the ancient Jewish method of doing biblical exegesis – not the dry academic stuff we do today that seldom moves or transforms anyone. A story or narrative captures the reader and pulls them into another world that may be utterly unlike their own. We could recount the life of Jesus in a non-story format. Let's try the curriculum vitae or resumé – we could list his words, deeds, and miracles with bullet points, dates, and names of witnesses. It would be technically correct, but it would engage, inspire, or transform no one.

We do not read the Gospels looking for information. We need to be willing to enter into Jesus' story, along with our own, allowing ourselves to be taken up and swept along by the narrative. This doesn't mean naively or uncritically, but with the openness and reverence appropriate to the message or Word contained in the text – and that Word is Jesus himself. We don't figure Jesus out or construct theories; we encounter him in the journey through the text.

We form our minds and hearts by our meditation on biblical wisdom. It can be called soul-making. There are general principles that tell us how to relate to people and to the world. Among them are justice, generosity, mercy and compassion, kindness, forgiveness, honesty and integrity, courage, and perseverance. There is nothing in Scripture about cloning, in vitro fertilization, nuclear war, climate change, or end-of-life issues. These are certainly important issues, but we cannot just flip open the Bible to the appropriate page and verse to address them. From the general principles contained in Scripture, we add prayer, reflection, dialogue – even with those we do not agree with – humility, tolerance, and a willingness to change our minds. We cannot take the shrill, dogmatic, easy way out. We dialogue with Scripture and with one another.

It is a common practice among more evangelically inclined Christians to guide their lives by the WWJD principle: What Would Jesus Do? This is valid up to a point, but many assume that Jesus would do what they do and would share their opinions and prejudices. Jesus seldom (if ever) talked about the things that upset us so often. He did not go around pointing out the sins of others; in fact, he gained a dark reputation for hanging around with those considered to be lowlifes and sinners. The closest Jesus came to anger and condemnation was his reaction to arrogance, self-righteousness, and the abuse of power. He commanded his followers not to chase after praise, honour, and prestige, and not to set themselves apart or lord it over others. Unfortunately, these teachings of the Lord often go unheeded. If we want to be serious about the WWJD principle, we should look carefully at the Jesus story. Jesus was unrelentingly merciful and compassionate. He empathized with human weakness, and gave people hope and encouragement. He called the best out of people and made it easy for them to want to do better. But mercy is threatening to some, and we can see this in the negative reaction of some Catholics to the teachings of Pope Francis on mercy.

In John 14, Jesus tells a bewildered Philip that if he has seen Jesus, he has seen the Father. Of course, this does not mean physical appearance. It could be rephrased to say, if you have encountered me, you have encountered God. In John, Jesus is the one filled with the spark of life and the living Spirit. In John 15, Jesus invited his followers to be his friends, rather than his servants. He assured them that if they were faithful to his commandment to love one another, both he and the Father would dwell within them, and they would dwell within Jesus and the Father. That is quite a promise – and it is one that has seldom really been taken seriously.

With that as our lens, we can approach the New Testament with an open heart and mind and enter into the story of Jesus. Then he will teach us to be what he is – the mercy and compassion of God.

For Further Reflection

1. The question of salvation has caused much controversy throughout the ages. How does the Bible address salvation? What does Jesus say? How does Jesus draw the teaching of the Old Testament into the teaching he shared with his followers? What is the message for you? How do you incorporate this teaching of Jesus in your daily life?

2. The toughest question of all is whether you are willing to enter into the Scriptures and allow yourself to be transformed by the Spirit. Are you willing to spend time in *lectio divina* or enter one of the parables or the nativity story or any other scene and experience the thoughts and feelings of the characters as they walk through that situation? Are you willing to meditate on the teachings of Jesus with an open heart and mind? How can you nourish this willingness so that Scripture can shape your life, your actions, your words?

Endnotes

Introduction

1 Alister McGrath, *In the Beginning: The Story of the King James Bible and How It Changed a Nation, a Language, and a Culture* (New York: Anchor, 2002), 1–2.

2 https://www.newsobserver.com/opinion/article213435679.html

3 Ibid.

Chapter 1

1 *Towne vs. Eisner*, 245 U.S. 418, 425 (7 January 1918). This was part of Holmes' argument in his interpretation of legal texts.

2 Joseph Fitzmyer, *The Interpretation of Scripture: In Defense of the Historical-Critical Method* (New York: Paulist Press, 2008). The first chapter contains a good history of Catholic biblical scholarship and the profound impact of *Divino Afflante Spiritu* and the Second Vatican Council on Catholic biblical scholarship.

3 A useful tool for this discussion is the document published by the Pontifical Biblical Commission: *Interpretation of the Bible in the Church* (Vatican City: Libreria Editrice Vaticana, 1993). All documents relating to Scripture study can be downloaded from http://catholic-resources.org/ChurchDocs.

4 *Verbum Domini.* Post-Synodal Apostolic Exhortation of Benedict XVI. See http://catholic-resources.org/ChurchDocs.

5 Many theologians have struck out in new directions. Elizabeth Johnson's *Creation and the Cross* is a good point of departure. One of the richest and most challenging is John Haught's *God After Darwin: A Theory of Evolution.* John Polkinghorne is an Anglican priest and an eminent scientist; he has written a number of books on science and faith. A helpful start would be his *Testing Scripture: A Scientist Explores the Bible.* Polkinghorne also co-authored with Nicholas Beale a very helpful book that explores evolution and other science/faith questions honestly and in a balanced manner: *Questions of Truth: Fifty-one Responses to Questions About God, Science, and Belief* (Louisville, KY: Westminster/John Knox Press, 2009).

6   Augustine of Hippo, *The Literal Meaning of Genesis*, John Taylor, trans. Ancient Christian Writers, vol. 41 (New York/Ramsey, NJ: Newman Press, 1982), 42–43. I.19.39.

7   Karen Armstrong, *The Battle for God* (New York: Ballantine, 2000), xvi–xvii.

Chapter 2

1   John J. Collins, *A Short Introduction to the Hebrew Bible*, 3rd ed. (Minneapolis, MN: Fortress Press, 2008). This is an excellent introduction to the Old Testament and the issues involved with interpretation.

2   Scholars use BCE – Before the Common Era – to designate the time before Christ, traditionally referred to as BC. The period after Christ – traditionally AD – is designated CE, or Common Era. This is a neutral way of referring to time periods that is more suitable in our multicultural and multi-religious world.

3   Eric A. Seibert, *The Violence of Scripture: Overcoming the Old Testament's Troubling Legacy* (Minneapolis, MN: Fortress, 2012), 1–2, 18.

4   Charles Kimball, *When Religion Becomes Evil* (San Francisco: HarperSanFrancisco, 2002). Kimball discusses these five warning signs that religion has become corrupted; see also Seibert, "Violence of Scripture," 15–25.

Chapter 3

1   German catechism *Grosser Gott Wir Loben Dich* 1940, quoted in Susannah Heschel, "When Jesus Was an Aryan," in *Betrayal: German Churches and the Holocaust* (Minneapolis, MN: Fortress Press, 1999), 68–89.

2   Second Vatican Council, *Nostra Aetate*, no. 4, http://www.vatican.va/archive/hist_councils/ii_vatican_council/documents/vat-ii_decl_19651028_nostra-aetate_en.html.

3   Pontifical Biblical Commission, *The Jewish People and Their Sacred Scriptures in the Christian Bible*, IV.B.86. http://www.vatican.va/roman_curia/congregations/cfaith/pcb_documents/rc_con_cfaith_doc_20020212_popolo-ebraico_en.html.

4   Mary C. Boys, *Has God Only One Blessing? Judaism as a Source of Christian Self-Understanding* (New York: Paulist Press, 2000), 8.

5   Pontifical Biblical Commission, *The Jewish People and Their Sacred Scriptures in the Christian Bible* (Vatican City: Libreria Editrice Vaticana, 2002).

6   Ibid.

7   Adela Yarbro Collings, *Crisis and Catharsis: The Power of the Apocalypse* (Philadelphia: Westminster Press, 1984), 111–38, 165–75.

8   Elisabeth Schüssler Fiorenza, *The Book of Revelation: Justice and Judgment*, 2nd ed. (Minneapolis, MN: Fortress, 1998), 7, 198.

9   Richard Bauckham, *The Theology of the Book of Revelation* (Cambridge: Cambridge University Press, 1993), 7, 18–19.

10 Scott M. Lewis, *What Are They Saying About New Testament Apocalyptic?* (New York/Mahwah, NJ: Paulist Press, 2004), 55.

11 Joseph Martos, *Doors of the Sacred: A Historical Introduction to Sacraments in the Catholic Church* (Liguori, MO: Liguori Publications, 2014), 54.

12 Ibid., 322–27.

Conclusion

1   The Tura Discovery of Manuscripts, http://www.tertullian.org/rpearse/manuscripts/tura_papyri.htm. Text: https://sites.google.com/site/demontortoise2000/Home/origen_dialog_with_heracleides.

Acknowledgements

I would like to express my appreciation for my New Testament students at Regis College, Toronto, over the years. It has been a privilege to exchange ideas with them.

I would also like to thank my editor at Novalis, Anne Louise Mahoney, for all her hard and careful work on the manuscript. Thanks also to Simon Appolloni at Novalis for the invitation and encouragement to write this book.

My thanks also go to Lynda Clayton and Sarah Rudolph for their feedback and helpful suggestions.

Scott Lewis, S.J.
September 30, 2019
Feast of St. Jerome